Guilford College, 1974–2020

Also by Richie Zweigenhaft

Co-authored with G. William Domhoff

Jews in the Protestant Establishment (Praeger, 1982)

Blacks in the White Establishment? A Study of Race and Class in America (Yale University Press, 1991)

Diversity in the Power Elite: Have Women and Minorities Reached the Top? (Yale University Press, 1998)

Blacks in the White Elite: Will the Progress Continue?, 2nd edition (Rowman & Littlefield, 2003)

Diversity in the Power Elite: How it Happened, Why it Matters, 2nd edition (Rowman & Littlefield, 2006)

The New CEOs: Women, African American, Latino, and Asian American Leaders of Fortune 500 Companies (Rowman & Littlefield, hardback, 2011, and paperback, with a new Introduction, 2014)

Diversity in the Power Elite: Ironies and Unfulfilled Promises, 3rd edition (Rowman & Littlefield, 2018)

Co-edited with Eugene Borgida

Collaboration in Psychological Science: Behind the Scenes (Worth, 2017)

GEEZERBALL: North Carolina Basketball at its Eldest (Sort of a Memoir) (Half Court Press, in cooperation with Scuppernong Books, 2019)

Jews, Palestinians, and Friends (Sort of a Memoir) (Half Court Press, in cooperation with Scuppernong Books, 2021)

Guilford College, 1974-2020

Sort of a Memoir in Two Parts

Richie Zweigenhaft

Half Court Press   Greensboro, N.C.

Second edition. First printing
ISBN 978-1-959104-00-1

DESIGN. Text in Minion Pro. Titles in
Carniola. Cover and interior design by
Andrew Saulters.

This book is produced by Half Court Press,
in cooperation with Scuppernong Books.

Guilford College, 1974–2020

Guilford College, 1974–2020

Introduction

Old Guy Sort of Writes His Memoirs

IT'S KIND OF A CLICHÉ—people get old, they retire, and they write their memoirs. It never crossed my mind that I would do that.

However, as I think back to what I have written over the last decade, even before I retired (in 2020 at the age of 75), the focus of some of my writing had shifted from more traditional social science articles and books based on empirical data, gathered and then massaged with the appropriate statistical analyses, to more personal accounts that looked backwards, not forwards. In 2014, as the result of a chance conversation with Brian Lampkin, the co-owner of Scuppernong, then a new independent bookstore in Greensboro, I learned that there were plans for a book of essays about Greensboro that would be titled *27 Views of Greensboro.* The editor of that volume was seeking submissions. I wrote a chapter titled "Gentrification and Its Discontents: Forty years in Fisher Park," about the changing nature of the neighborhood I had lived in since 1975, and my reactions to these changes. The editor liked it, and it was included in the book.[1]

1. Zweigenhaft, Richie (2015). "Gentrification and its discontents: Forty Years in Fisher Park." In Woodman, Elizabeth (Ed.), *27 Views of Greensboro: The Gate city in Prose and Poetry.* Hillsborough, NC: Eno Publications, pp. 64–68.

In 2017, I co-edited a book with Gene Borgida, a college friend who teaches psychology at the University of Minnesota, titled *Collaboration in Psychological Science: Behind the Scenes.*[2] This was a traditional academic project—we cajoled eminent psychologists who had collaborated extensively in their careers to write essays about their experiences working with one another, and with others (both good and bad). We found a publisher, we got the authors to submit their essays, we edited these essays, we read the galley proofs, and we then tried to convince the marketing folks to promote the book. Gene and I co-authored introductory and concluding chapters for that volume. All very academic. But the genesis of the project, way back in 2011 (I was a mere 66 at the time) was a book I bought at a used bookstore in Asheville by Tom Grimes titled *Mentor: A Memoir.*[3] Reading Grimes' account of his mentor at the Iowa Writer's Workshop led me to think about my mentor—a faculty member when I was a graduate student, who subsequently became an academic collaborator and a good friend. I wrote a draft of what ultimately became one of the chapters in the book on collaboration, and in it I looked back on my experiences over more than five decades collaborating with various colleagues, but especially with that mentor, G. William Domhoff, with whom by then I had coauthored many books and articles.[4]

Almost two years before I actually retired, at dinner one night with some friends, after I mentioned that I had played basketball on campus that day in what had come to be known as

2. Zweigenhaft, Richard L. and Borgida, E. (Eds.), (2017). *Collaboration in Psychological Science: Behind the Scenes.* New York: Worth.

3. Grimes, Tom (2010). *Mentor: A Memoir.* Portland, OR: Tin House.

4. Zweigenhaft, Richard L. (2017). "Studying diversity in the American power structure, collaboratively." In Zweigenhaft, R. L. and Borgida, E. (Eds.), *Collaboration in Psychological Science: Behind the Scenes.* New York: Worth, pp. 175–187.

"the geezer game," one of these friends (Kathy Adams, also my neighbor and longtime departmental colleague), encouraged me to write a book about the noontime game. She knew that it had been going for a long time—it started in 1976—and she thought I should write a history of the game, with emphasis on how it had lasted so long. It was summertime, so I had no classes to teach, and my wife was visiting her sister in California. For the next week I found myself banging away on the computer about the origins of the game, and thinking more fully about the reasons that it had lasted for more than four decades. When months later I had a complete draft, and needed some feedback, Michael Gaspeny, a longtime friend, who played in the game when he taught at Guilford, encouraged me to put more of myself in the narrative. In that early draft that he read, I had included some personal commentary in footnotes. He suggested that I expand on them and elevate them from footnotes into the text. He didn't quite call for a memoir, but he thought I should play more of a role in the story I was telling. When the time came to decide on a title, after considering many options, and after a key suggestion from my cousin Mark, I chose to call it *GEEZERBALL: North Carolina Basketball at its Eldest (Sort of a Memoir)*. The book was published in February 2020, about a month before COVID swept the nation.

When COVID hit, I was about to turn 75. I had been thinking about retiring, but was still teaching and very much enjoying it. In fact, I was teaching an interdisciplinary seminar for seniors titled "The American Upper Class" that was one of the best classes I had taught in decades. In March, my classes, like all the other classes at Guilford, went online. Even before the pandemic hit, Guilford was struggling economically, and I feared that the double whammy of ongoing economic woes plus COVID meant that some of my colleagues, much younger than I, were going to be laid off. For all three reasons—turning

75, having to teach online, and fearing that colleagues would be laid off—I decided to retire.

So there I was, a retired guy, socially isolated along with the rest of the country, with time on my hands. I didn't exactly decide to write my memoirs—as I have indicated, I had started to write retrospectively for almost a decade, about my neighborhood, about my collaborative academic work, and about the geezer game. One day, while riding my bike (the geezer game was done, though, as will be seen in the Epilogue to Part Two of this book, it came back), it occurred to me that I might have been the first Jew hired to a tenure track position at Guilford College, back in 1974. Over the next few months, I began to write, first about my arrival at Guilford, and the subsequent hiring of a number of other Jewish faculty, and this led me to think about, and write about, the complex relationships between Jews and Quakers, and, increasingly over time, among Jews, Quakers, and Palestinians. What emerged was a book published in September 2021 titled *Jews, Palestinians, and Friends: 45 Years at a Quaker College (Sort of a Memoir)*. As with *GEEZERBALL*, it was in part an institutional history, albeit an idiosyncratic one, and it included my own experiences and observations (thus, sort of a memoir).

During my first year of retirement, 2020-2021, Guilford College underwent an alarming but also remarkable transformation. The President announced that she was going to take a year-long leave, and then retire from the presidency, and over the next year she was followed by two interim presidents. Many faculty and staff did indeed lose their jobs, and termination letters were mailed to 27 faculty, 16 of whom were tenured. A group of passionate alumni organized to save the college (the group called itself Save Guilford College), and, at least for the time being, did so (the faculty who had received termination letters were not fired, though some decided to go elsewhere).

Though retired, I continued to work with the revitalized chapter of the American Association of University Professors (AAUP), a group that played a key role in helping to redirect the school from the disastrous course it was on. I decided to write about what had taken place, with a focus on the organizing and activism of the AAUP, and I published an article about this in a journal called *Academe*.[5] I then decided to include an expanded version of this article as a new, final, chapter of a second edition of *Jews, Palestinians, and Friends* (as one reader pointed out, this new final chapter was not really about Jews, Palestinians, and Quakers, but it seemed a good place to tell this story). This second edition was published in October 2021.

Meanwhile, vaccines had been developed for COVID, and boosters as well, and the number of cases and deaths had subsided. By the fall of 2021, the college was holding in-person classes again, though masks were still required, and some faculty chose to continue to teach online. Some of my basketball buddies and I started playing outside in May 2021, and we were still doing so in November, but it was getting cold. After many emails back and forth, we were allowed back in the gym at Guilford in February 2022 (for the first seven weeks, masks were required). I decided to write an epilogue to *GEEZERBALL* updating the return of the inside game at Guilford. When I consulted my editor and fellow ballplayer, Brian Lampkin, about a second edition of *GEEZERBALL*, he suggested combining the two "sort of memoirs" into a single book, one that would include the two accounts that focus on slices of life at Guilford College over the past 45 years or so, along with the updates I wrote for each.

So here it is, an old guy's "sort of memoir," my take on relations among three groups (Jews, Palestinians and Quakers)

5. Zweigenhaft, R. (2022). "How the AAUP helped to save Guilford College," *Academe. 108* (1), 39–45.

at Guilford College over a 45-year period, and how the AAUP and a group called Save Guilford College helped the school change directions from the disastrous course it was on (in Part One) and the story of the geezer game, before and after COVID, with a focus on how the game has managed to last for so long (in Part Two).

Part One

Jews, Palestinians, and Friends

45 Years at a Quaker College

(Sort of a Memoir)

To Jonathan, Diya, and Max (Jew, Palestinian, Friend)

And Lisa (by my side for all 45 years)

I   *Jews of Many Persuasions*

I ARRIVED AT GUILFORD COLLEGE in the fall of 1974, a highly assimilated Jew. I grew up in the D.C. area, was bar mitzvahed in 1958 in a conservative synagogue, but when I came to Greensboro I had not set foot in a synagogue in years. I had spent the previous four years in Santa Cruz, California, the two before that in Corning, New York, and the year before that in New York City. I don't recall being in a synagogue in any of those three places.

I was, however, and remain, very much Jewish in the cultural sense that includes lots of warm and highly verbal relatives, lox, cream cheese and bagels, an appreciation for Mel Brooks and Woody Allen movies, and wariness around people who are quite sure that Jesus was the messiah. In fact, as I finished work on my Ph.D., I did not plan on applying to any teaching jobs at religious schools, but my experiences with Quakers in the anti-war movement during the late 1960s and early 1970s had been positive, so I thought I might be able to tolerate, and be tolerated by, Quakers. I therefore applied to, and was hired by, Guilford College, a Quaker-affiliated school.

I received three warnings about Guilford and Greensboro. The first came in November 1973, a few days before Guilford flew me to North Carolina for my interview. I called my friend Sylvia who at the time was the only person I knew from North Carolina. Sylvia grew up in Burlington, went to Duke, and then moved immediately (and forevermore) to New York City, which is where I met her, in 1965. When I asked her what she knew about Guilford College, she warned me that when she was growing up in Burlington it was a quite conservative school, and Greensboro also was pretty conservative. She worried that I might not fit in very well. She encouraged me to watch the local TV news during my visit.

The second warning came months later, in June 1974, after I had been offered and accepted the job at Guilford, as Lisa (soon to be my wife), Throckmorton (legendary first dog) and I were about to leave Santa Cruz to drive across country. A Jewish friend of ours, a lawyer who grew up in New York City, made a more dire prediction, this one taking into account not only that I was liberal, but also that I was Jewish: "Richie," he warned me one day as he was teaching me to play stickball on a racquetball court, "you're going to have a cross burned on your front lawn!"

The third warning, this one from a stranger, came a few weeks later, on our trip across country. We had visited friends in Albuquerque, and, since it was about 105 degrees in the shade in Albuquerque, we decided to drive north to Aspen to see some other friends and for some cooler weather before heading across the interminable Midwest. Almost to Aspen, we stopped at a peak to watch the sun go down, and there was another couple there who had stopped for the same reason. When they asked us where we were from (Santa Cruz, California), and where we were going (Greensboro, North Carolina), the guy shook his head and said, "You're going the wrong way."

When we arrived, however, we could not have received a warmer reception from people at the college or from the neighbors in Lake Daniel, our new neighborhood. Moreover, we were quite surprised by how visible and even prominent Jews had been in Greensboro. There were libraries, roads, and even a hospital that I assumed had been named after Jewish people (Moses Cone!). This led me to write a series of articles, first on the local Jewish community, then on the Jews in nearby Winston-Salem, then on Jews throughout the South, and ultimately, a book titled *Jews in the Protestant Establishment*. I used to jokingly refer to myself as a Jewologist, a term that made some people nervous, although I was perhaps off the hook, but maybe not, when a character in a Philip Roth novel was referred to as a Jewologist.[1]

In contrast to what I found in Greensboro, Jews were not all that visible at Guilford College. There may not have been any Jews employed by the school, though two of my colleagues seemed kind of Jewish to me—at least they triggered the Jewish equivalent of gaydar (let's call it Jewdar). One was Ted Benfey, a distinguished professor of chemistry. Ted's story, I was later to learn, was quite remarkable. He was born in Berlin to a prominent though highly assimilated Jewish family. His father, trained as a lawyer, had become a supreme court justice, and his mother's family ran what Chris Benfey, Ted's son, has described

1. Zweigenhaft, Richard L. and G. William Domhoff. 1982. *Jews in the Protestant Establishment*. New York: Praeger. In his 19th book, published in 1993, *Operation Shylock: A Confession* (New York: Simon and Schuster), Philip Roth, the author of the book, uses the term "Jewologist" to describe Philip Roth, a character in the book, as "a leading Jewologist of international literature" (p. 334). Whereas Philip Roth was a "Jewologist of international literature," I considered myself a Jewologist who sought sociological, or maybe social psychological, understanding. Fictional or real, I considered Roth a kindred spirit.

as "the biggest and wealthiest publishing empire in all of Europe." Ted's father, however, had converted to Lutheranism, as Chris explained, "both for patriotic reasons—to feel more German—and to advance his judicial career." His mother's family had been baptized late in the 19th century. But, again to quote from Chris Benfey, "To Hitler...they were all Jews." In an essay that he wrote in 2009 titled "Getting out of Nazi Germany," Ted made it clear that Hitler's views had permeated the culture: "My classmates were taunting me for being Jewish. The fact that we were Lutherans made no difference." Hitler seized the publishing house in 1933, Ted's father was fired in 1935, and in 1936, shortly before his 11th birthday, Ted left Germany to live in England with friends of the Benfey family who had emigrated from Berlin a year or two earlier.

During the war years in London, he and the family he lived with became Quakers. As he recalls, the only Lutheran church was in the center of the city, and they were living on the outskirts, so they attended the local Church of England. There, however, the sermons "became more patriotically hate-filled rather than loving so we slowly migrated to the Quakers." At the age of 21, with a Ph.D. in organic chemistry, he came to the United States for a research fellowship at Columbia University, and this led in 1948 to a job teaching at Haverford College. While there, he met and subsequently married Rachel Thomas who was teaching at the Haverford Friends School (she had become a Quaker while an undergraduate at Guilford College). Ted's parents and siblings were able to leave Germany, but he lost family members to the Holocaust.[2] It was, therefore, easy enough for me to spot Ted's assimilated German Jewish roots, but he was not Jewish—he was a Quaker.

2. Benfey, Theodor. 2018. "Getting out of Nazi Germany," in Benfey, Theodor (Ed), *The Experience of War: Residents of Friends Homes and Their Families Tell Their Stories*. Greensboro, NC, pp. 52-55; the quote

The other person who got my Jewdar going was Adele Groulx, who was born Adele Freedman and, after divorcing her first husband, Aimé Groulx, and marrying Jeff Wayman (both goys), was later to be known as Adele Wayman. Adele grew up in Greensboro (a townie!) to Jewish parents. Her parents were members of the reform congregation, Temple Emanuel. Like most Jewish girls of her generation, she was not bat mitzvahed when she was 13, but she was confirmed at the age of 16. Then, after four years at Vassar, her marriage to Aimé, and her own spiritual yearnings that led her to attend a Quaker meeting for five or six years when she first started teaching at Guilford, to regular participation for a few years in a campus group that performed a Buddhist ceremony in the Zen tradition, then to visit a Buddhist retreat center outside Asheville, NC, quite a few times, as well as later attending a conference on witchcraft, she had pretty much left behind whatever formal ties to Judaism she once had. When I asked one of Adele's long-time colleagues "if you had to say what religion Adele is, in 10 words or fewer, what would you say?" his response was "Hard to pin down—Jewish/ Buddhist/New Age?" When I asked Adele the same question, she said "For 30 years or more, I have been a serious meditator,

about his classmates is on p. 52; Benfey, Christopher. 2012. *Red Brick, Black Mountain, White Clay: Reflections on Art, Family, & Survival.* New York: Penguin, 2012, pp. 73-82; the quoted passages are on p. 79.

In 1939, Guilford hired J. Curt Victorius to teach Economics. Like Ted Benfey, he was born in Germany to Jewish parents, and like Ted's parents, Curt and his wife, Gertud, in an effort to avoid the increasing German anti-Semitism, converted to Lutheranism. And, like Ted Benfey, Curt and Gertrud became Quakers. They were members of New Garden Friends Meeting and are buried in the New Garden Cemetery. See Beal, Gertrude and Max Carter. 2019. *Stories from a Quaker Graveyard.* Greensboro, NC: The New Garden Cemetery Association, pp. 33-34.

mostly Zen, and experimenting with Tibetan Buddhism" (more than ten words, but you get the drift).[3] Still, when I met Adele, and certainly when I met her parents (Arthur and Rose Freedman), I knew that like me, beneath that assimilated surface, she was Jewish. But like Ted Benfey, and unlike me, she no longer considers herself to be Jewish.

In his engaging and informative book about living in and visiting Palestine over the last five decades, *Palestine and Israel: A Personal Encounter*, Max Carter, a birthright Quaker who was the campus minister at Guilford from 1990 until he retired in 2015, refers to a Guilford student as a "Jewish Quaker."[4] He doesn't define this term (are there Episcopalian Quakers? Baptist Quakers? Muslim Quakers?), and I take it to mean someone who was raised as a Jew and does not reject that Jewish heritage and training, but who has been drawn to Quakerism, and perhaps even has formally joined a Quaker meeting.[5] Quakers, like Jews, come in different categories. Whereas the traditional sects of Jews are Orthodox, Conservative and

3. This quote from Adele and much of the information in this paragraph are from a phone interview with her on May 4, 2020.

4. Carter, Max L. 2020. *Palestine and Israel: A Personal Encounter*, Newberg, OR: Barclay Press, pp. 142 and 146.

5. When one formally joins a Quaker meeting, one is considered a "convinced Quaker" (as opposed to a "birthright Quaker"). For Jews, and most other religions, the person would be referred to as a "convert" to Judaism. A person who converts to Judaism from, say, Catholicism or some form of Protestantism, not only has left the previous religion behind for the new one, but in the case of Judaism the converts are often more committed to the observance of Jewish practices than those born into Jewish families.

When I asked Marie Branson Knapp, a Guilford alum ('83) if she was, as I recalled, a birthright Quaker, she responded that she was but that "that title has always sounded so divisive." I wrote her back and asked, "You think it is any more divisive than 'the Chosen People?'"

Reform, and now there are various other sects, such as those who call themselves Reconstructionist Jews and Humanistic Jews, Quakers can be Evangelical, Conservative, or Liberal. The first two categories assume, maybe require, a belief in Christ's divinity, but the third does not, so perhaps one can be a Jewish Liberal Quaker, but not a Jewish Evangelical Quaker or a Jewish Conservative Quaker. In any event, I doubt that Ted Benfey ever called himself a Jewish Quaker, though maybe he did in the early years of his transition, and Adele Wayman certainly didn't, as Quakerism wasn't where she chose to go (though she spent some time there along the way).

I myself am definitely Jewish, and definitely not a Quaker, but in some of my best moments in the Guilford community I have been described as "Quakeresque" or "Quakerly" by some birthright Quakers with impeccable credentials. Still, now that I think back, even though I was and am an assimilated and unobservant Jew, and though I was not and am not a Jewish Quaker, I think that I was one of the first two full-time tenure-track Guilford College faculty members to call ourselves Jewish—the other was Sheridan Simon, hired in the physics department at the same time I was.

In this brief account, sort of a memoir, sort of a slice of Guilford College history, I hope to address two topics. The first is to explore the dramatic transition Guilford made from an all-white conservative school to one that diversified its faculty, its student body, and its board of trustees, and became known as a liberal and progressive college. The second examines how the increased attention on the campus to Middle East politics, especially the conflicts between Israel and Palestine, led to some divisions on the campus, but, much more problematically, to a major chasm between the college and the local Jewish community.

Sheridan and I were not the only Jewish faculty members for long. In my second year at the college, we hired two more full-fledged happy-to-call-themselves Jews. Through an unexpected confluence of events, I had become chair of the psychology department, and I chaired a search that led us to hire two women, one of whom, Jackie Ludel, was Jewish (the other, Claire Morse, was definitely not). Jackie, born and raised in Queens, New York, was my age (past tense here, as she died in 2017). Like me, and like many, maybe most of the Jews of our generation, she was Jewish but not observant, and, like me, she did not join either of the two congregations here in Greensboro.

That year the college also hired a Jewish couple. Jonathan Malino was hired to teach in the Philosophy Department and his wife, Sarah, when she completed her Ph.D. in history, joined the History Department. This was a Jewish couple who were really Jewish, not the unacknowledged (like Ted and Adele) or the unobservant (like me and Jackie), but the real deal. Jonathan, the son of a prominent reform rabbi, and an ordained rabbi himself, holds a Ph.D. in philosophy from Columbia University and a rabbinical degree from Hebrew Union College; Sarah, whose Ph.D. in history was, like Jonathan's, from Columbia, met Jonathan when he was an undergraduate at Brandeis (a school that real Jews went to) and she was at Wellesley. Because Jonathan was a rabbi, he was given a courtesy appointment to Temple Emanuel, where he assisted the rabbi there for nine years, and then when a rabbi that Jonathan and Sarah liked and admired was hired at the synagogue, they joined it—so they were members of both congregations here in town. The Malinos hosted Passover seders and break-the-fast events, and not only did both of their sons have bar mitzvahs, their daughter had a bat mitzvah and subsequently became a rabbi (she is a third-generation rabbi, but the first woman rabbi in the family).

So, five real Jews in two years! What brought this about? Many factors may have been at play. One might have been that the year I was hired, the college had for the first time recruited nationally, not just regionally. That meant that instead of advertising regionally, and interviewing applicants who were in North Carolina or nearby states, the school conducted a national search. When I came to campus for a memorable day and a half of interviews with faculty, students, and administrators, I might have been the first person to be brought for an interview from the west coast.

Another factor, not unrelated to the first, is that Grimsley Hobbs was the president of the school. Grimsley, a birthright Quaker whose grandfather, Lewis Lyndon Hobbs, was the first President of Guilford College (from 1888-1915), grew up in Chapel Hill, and in his teen-age years went off to attend George School, a Quaker boarding school outside Philadelphia. One of his friends at George School was a Jewish kid from Wilmington, NC, named Arthur Bluethenthal. They both were on the wrestling team (Grimsley, who was 6'5," wrestled heavyweight, and Arthur, who was 5'6," wrestled at one of the lightest weights). It may have been unusual for a Jewish kid from Wilmington to attend George School, but it has not been unusual for Jewish kids to attend Quaker schools. In fact, at times some of the Quaker schools in the Philadelphia area have had more Jewish students than Quaker students. An oft-cited joke about the make-up of these schools is that Friends schools are places where Episcopalian faculty teach Jewish students how to be Quakers.

In 1950, nine years after he graduated from George School, Arthur and his wife Joanne (nee Kapnek, also Jewish) moved to Greensboro. Therefore, when Grimsley accepted the job as President of Guilford in 1965 (and he and his wife Lois Ann left Earlham College to move to Greensboro), he had at least one good friend in his new hometown: his prep school wrestling buddy, Arthur Bluethenthal.

When Grimsley arrived, Guilford was very much the small conservative school that my friend Sylvia recalled. In 1955, for example, a faculty committee had recommended that the school's athletic teams not compete against integrated teams. The committee's reasoning went as follows: "The committee deems it generally inadvisable at this time to arrange for or engage in competitive contests with teams of other races. We believe it would be detrimental…to force upon the constituency of our sponsoring body and the community in which we are situated any inter group or interracial policies for which they do not seem prepared." The committee was no doubt aware of the views of the board of trustees, especially Robert Frazier. Frazier, a lawyer, succeeded his father on the board in 1932 and he remained on the board for the next 37 years, serving as chair from 1950-1969. He was clearly a force to be reckoned with—he also was the Mayor of the township called Guilford College from 1951-1955, and (presumably demonstrating his belief in keeping education, as the segregationists used to say, "separate but equal") a member of the board of trustees at North Carolina A&T, a historically black university, from 1951 through 1973, and the chair of that board from 1957-1969. In 1958, one member of Guilford's board wrote to another that "I definitely think this matter of integration, about which there seems to be much hysteria, at this time does not have a place in the constructive thinking of the school, and I want to leave it out of the picture." In 1959, Clyde Milner, Guilford's president, said "Negro students would not be accepted until the board of trustees as a body was willing to accept them."

The result of these views held by Robert Frazier and others on the board of trustees, and these timid responses by the faculty and the president, was, as Guilford Quaker archivist Gwen Erickson concludes in her article on "Race Relations at Guilford College," that "Guilford was by no means a leader in integration. The last of the Quaker-founded colleges to allow African American students, Guilford integrated around the same time as most other denominational colleges in North Carolina (and years after leaders within the state)."[6]

By the time Grimsley and Lois Ann arrived in 1965, Arthur and Joanne had been in Greensboro for fifteen years, and they had become pillars of the Greensboro Jewish community. They were members of Temple Emanuel, and Arthur had been the president of the congregation and on the board of directors. Three years into his presidency, in 1968, Grimsley hired Arthur to establish a wrestling team at Guilford, which Arthur then coached for five years, from 1968 to 1973. Joanne not only was active in the temple, she also was active in the wider community, and as William Chafe notes in his seminal book about the integration of the public schools in Greensboro, *Civilities and Civil Rights: Greensboro, North Carolina, and the Black Struggle for Freedom*, she was an important community leader when it came to the integration of schools in Greensboro.[7]

6. Erickson, Gwen. "Race Relations at Guilford College," Digital Collections, UNCG. http://libcdm1.uncg.edu/cdm/essayguilford/collection/CivilRights; see also Stoesen, Alexander R. 1987. *Guilford College: On the Strength of 150 Years*, Greensboro, NC: Guilford College. Stoesen limits his critique of Frazier, the person who was probably more responsible than anyone else for the college's delayed integration, to the following: "A determined and strong-willed man, Frazier gave massive amounts of time and energy to Guilford, although if law was involved he charged for it" (p. 134).

7. Chafe, William H. 1981. *Civilities and Civil Rights: Greensboro, North Carolina, and the Black Struggle for Freedom.* New York: Oxford University Press. In his book, Chafe thanks Joanne Bluethenthal "for her willingness to let me peruse the wealth of material that she has collected over the years about the final desegregation fight in Greensboro between 1969 and 1972" (p. 420). In 2016, a few years after Arthur Bluethenthal died, the family gave $100,000 to the college to pay for the cost of construction of two new tennis courts that are now part of the ten-court complex on the northwest corner of the campus.

Maybe Grimsley's boyhood and then adult friendship with Arthur, or the Hobbs' friendship with the Bluethenthals, contributed to Guilford finally hiring some actual Jews on the faculty (five in a two-year period!). Maybe it was the decision to do national searches, or it was simply that the time had come, and it was part of the regional as well as national Zeitgeist. In the first few years of Grimsley's presidency, he hired faculty who were very much a part of the transition that changed Guilford from a conservative and quite regional college to the progressive institution with a national reputation that it was to become. In 1966 alone, the college hired Jerry Godard (as Executive Dean, but also with an appointment in Psychology), Cyril Harvey (birthright Quaker) in Geology, Beth Keiser in English, Mel Keiser (birthright Quaker) in Religious Studies, Claude Chauvigne (later Mourot-Hoffman) in French, and Jim McMillan, an African American, in Art (so, notably, Guilford hired its first African American faculty member eight years before it hired its first Jew). These then-young faculty members, some of whom had followed Grimsley from Earlham to Guilford, surely had spent some time with Jews and, like Grimsley, probably had some childhood friends who were Jewish. In the obituary that she wrote for the local newspaper in 1990 when Grimsley died, at the age of 67, in an automobile accident that was perhaps caused by Grimsley having had a heart attack, Kathy Coe, a former journalist and at the time a member of the board of trustees, did not mention the fact that late in his presidency Guilford hired some Jewish faculty, but she did give him credit for diversifying the faculty: "Hobbs set out to rebuild the faculty. He recognized new demands for diversity in college teaching. He lobbied for higher tuition to pay higher teacher salaries and attracted top teachers to Guilford from across the country. He gave them a greater role in campus decisions than the faculty had ever had."[8]

Grimsley Hobbs also played a key role in diversifying the board of trustees. When Grimsley became president, Robert Frazier had been on the board for 33 years, and had been the chair for fifteen years. Not only had Frazier resisted the integration of the student body, but he insisted that all members of the board had to be Quakers. Grimsley argued that it was important to open the board up, and, especially, to include prominent members of the Greensboro community. As Lois Ann Hobbs recounted to me in an email: "Right from the beginning Grimsley opposed this [an exclusively Quaker board] as restricting it from powerful members of the community. It soon came down as a showdown, either G. or R. would have to go." Grimsley won that battle. Robert Frazier—a man who was used to getting his way—began to boycott board meetings, was removed as chairman, and then resigned. As a result of winning this battle, Grimsley not only helped to oust Frazier from power at Guilford (perhaps one of Grimsley's most important accomplishments) but he also paved the way for Stanley Frank, a prominent member of the local Jewish community, to join the board.[9]

Stanley Frank served on the board for 36 years. When he died, in January 2006, there was a funeral service at Temple Emanuel. After that service, on the way to the Hebrew Cemetery, the funeral procession stopped at Guilford College where a small crowd of faculty and staff had assembled outside the Frank Family Science Center, a building that Stanley and

8. Coe, Kathy. Nov. 20, 1990. "Grimsley T. Hobbs," *Greensboro News & Record.* https://www.greensboro.com/grimsley-t-hobbs/article_6983d53d-77ae-586f-b1b2-9cf747546d39.html

9. Email from Lois Ann Hobbs (age 98!), May 27, 2020.

his wife Dorothy had helped to fund. Jonathan Malino chanted a prayer (El Maleh Rachamin, a prayer for the departed).[10]

I am convinced that another person also was key to Guilford hiring five Jewish faculty between 1974 and 1976. By 1974, Bruce Stewart was running the school on a day-to-day basis. Grimsley could be socially awkward, but Bruce was able to connect with anyone. Bruce had grown up in Lynn, MA, in a working-class family (his father, a Scottish immigrant, attended school only through the third grade). As the result of a chance encounter with J. Floyd "Pete" Moore, a Guilford College faculty member who was in Boston doing graduate work at Boston University, Bruce came to Guilford on a scholarship (apparently when Pete encouraged him to consider Guilford College, a Quaker school in North Carolina, Bruce's response was "Where's that, and what's a Quaker?").[11] He graduated in 1962, earned a master's from UNC, worked at Page High School during the early years of that school's integration, and then, after a stint in Winston-Salem at the N. C. School of the Arts, returned to work at Guilford in 1967, and over the next 13 years served the college in a variety of capacities. When I say a variety of capacities, I mean it: at various times Bruce was the Director of Admissions, the Director of the Richardson Fellows Program, Assistant to the President, Acting Academic Dean, Interim Provost, and then, from 1979 through 1984, he was Provost and Associate to the President for Development.

10. Jarboe, Michelle. 2006. "'Advocate' Laid to Rest." *Greensboro News & Record*, January 5. https://www.greensboro.com/news/advocate-laid-to-rest/article_76fe8803-1ece-52f2-93d2-684413459777.html

11. Schlosser, Jim. January 13, 2009. "Guilford Grad Leads School Obama Girls are Attending," *Greensboro News & Record*, https://www.greensboro.com/news/columnists/guilford-grad-leads-school-obama-girls-are-attending/article_6340bdf0-3bf4-5fce-bba6-6515c2324151.html

When I spent that day and a half on the campus for my interviews in November 1973, I think Bruce's title was Assistant to the President, and he was effectively the primary administrator on campus. Grimsley was much less visible; in fact, he was not on campus when I visited, and Bruce interviewed me. I know that a little over two years later, when we hired Jackie Ludel and Jonathan Malino, Bruce interviewed both of them (maybe Grimsley did, but maybe not), and he was very taken by how brilliant he thought Jackie and Jonathan were (he was right). When Grimsley retired, in 1980, Bruce applied for but was not selected as the next president (the board chose Bill Rogers as its sixth president). In 1984, Bruce left to become the Headmaster at Abington Friends, a Quaker prep school outside Philadelphia, and then, 14 years later, he became Head at Sidwell Friends, the elite Quaker prep school in Washington, D.C., that has educated the children of many prominent D.C. residents, including the children of Al Gore and the Obamas. When Bruce remarried (he and his first wife had divorced some years earlier), although he had become a convinced Quaker back in the early 1980s, and regularly attended meetings in Abington and while at Sidwell Friends, he married Andra Jurist, a Jewish woman.

So maybe the somewhat sudden arrival of five Jews here in Quakerland happened because Guilford did national searches, maybe it was because Grimsley had a longtime Jewish friend going back to his prep school days, and was open to breaking what may or may not have been seen as a barrier, and maybe it was because Bruce and the new wave of faculty that Grimsley, Bruce, and Jerry Godard had hired were intent on bringing the best possible faculty to the college (I suspect it was Bruce's decision to do national searches).

In any event, the doors were open, and although Jews did not exactly flood in, or take over the place, they kept coming. Roy

Nydorf was hired to teach in the art department in 1978, but then, as far as I can tell, for the next 25 years or so no full-time tenure track Jewish people were hired (there were probably some Jews who were hired as part-time adjunct faculty, and definitely one, Jeffrey Janowitz, my colleague in the psychology department, who was full-time but not tenure track).[12]

The college did hire a Jewish Academic Dean. In 1981, I was asked to chair a search committee for a new Academic Dean. This ended up taking two years. In the first year, we selected John Stoneburner to serve as the Interim Dean. John, the son of a minister, had attended Earlham College, a Quaker school, where he roomed with Mel Keiser, and the two of them were later to become colleagues in Guilford's Religious Studies department when John was hired in 1968. Although John was not a card-carrying Quaker, he and his wife Carol sometimes attended New Garden Friends Meeting; he was, however, very Quakerly, or Quakeresque (take your pick). The search committee that I chaired decided to recommend him to the college's newly hired but not-yet-arrived president, Bill Rogers, who was still living in Cambridge, MA, months away from officially beginning work as Guilford's sixth president. Bill accepted our recommendation to hire John over the other two candidates, both of whom were birthright Quakers (Cyrus Johnson, sociology, and Elwood Parker, math).

12. Jeffrey was not just Jewish, he was the son of Holocaust survivors.

Notably, in 1977, when Davidson College was about to hire its first Jewish faculty member, he refused to sign a document that required him to pledge "to uphold and to increase Davidson's effectiveness as a church-related college." This "Christian tenure policy" shocked many at the school and in the community, led to national coverage, and Davidson soon changed the policy. At the time Davidson, with a student body of 1,300, had six Jewish students. See "College withdraws job offer to a Jew, touching off furor," *New York Times*, May 1, 1977, p. 31.

The following year we did a national search. John, as Interim Dean, was the inside candidate. We brought three others to the campus to interview, one of whom, Sam Schuman, who was Jewish, came from the University of Maine, Orono. After what can only be described as extensive and contentious deliberations (this was one of the two hardest committees I was on in my 45 years at Guilford—the other, in 1998, was usually referred to as the "downsizing committee," though it had a less ominous official name), the committee recommended to Bill Rogers, just finishing his first semester on campus, that the college hire Sam. Bill accepted our recommendation (usually when I tell the story of this search committee, especially the second year and its aftermath, I refer to Dylan's great album title, and great album, "Blood on the Tracks"). Sam became the first Jew in a senior administrative position at Guilford.[13]

Both of Sam's parents were Jewish and members of a reform congregation in a suburb outside Chicago, he was bar mitzvahed, he remained active in various Jewish youth group organizations throughout high school, and for a while he even contemplated becoming a rabbi. While an undergraduate at Grinnell he met Nancy, the non-Jewish woman he was to marry, and when they came to Greensboro with their two children, the family did not join either the temple or the synagogue. They celebrated both Jewish and Christian holidays, and neither of the children identified as Jewish. Sam stayed at Guilford for ten

13. There have been a few other Jews in senior administrative positions, though none as senior as Sam's roles—when he arrived his title was Academic Dean and when he left he was the Vice President for Academic Affairs. The three who come to mind are Sybille Colby, Dean for Continuing Education, for two years in the 1970s, Rita Serotkin, who was the Associate Vice President and Dean for Continuing Education from 2006 to 2015, and Barb Boyette, Associate Academic Dean for Academic Support from 2008 to 2017.

years before he went on to serve as Chancellor at the University of North Carolina, Asheville (UNCA). While in Asheville he joined a reform congregation and periodically attended Friday night services. He left Asheville to become the Chancellor at the University of Minnesota, Morris. In a book that Sam wrote titled *Seeing the Light: Religious Colleges in the Twenty-First Century*, he described his background as "Jewish faith, political liberal, theologically conflicted."[14] When he died in 2014, my wife, Lisa (whose father was Jewish but whose mother was not[15]), who had become a hospital chaplain after a two-decade career as a potter and teaching ceramics and drawing at Guilford, conducted the memorial service at Sam and Nancy's Asheville home.

Between 1974 and 2020, the college hired enough Jews, I believe, for a minyan. For you gentiles out there, a minyan is the quorum of ten Jewish people over the age of 13 who are required for traditional public worship. As with so many things,

---

14. Schuman, Samuel. 2010. *Seeing the Light: Religious Colleges in the Twenty-First Century.* Baltimore, MD: Johns Hopkins University Press, p. 17.

15. According to Orthodox and Conservative Jews, including the Conservative synagogue in which I grew up, if the mother is not Jewish, the child is not considered Jewish (my Conservative childhood rabbi would not marry me and Lisa because her mother was not Jewish, even though her father was Jewish and she identified as Jewish). Reform congregations have concluded that if either parent is Jewish, that's good enough for them. Whether one is Jewish or not also depends on who is asking, and what their criteria are. As Chris Benfey wrote about his father's situation in Germany in 1935, even though Ted's father had become a Lutheran and Ted's mother's family had been baptized, "To Hitler...they were all Jews." One of the corporate executives I interviewed for *Jews in the Protestant Establishment*, Laurence Tisch, whose family owned CBS and the New York Yankees (and more), made the same point to me: "When Hitler came around he didn't ask questions whether you were or you weren't—it wasn't what you said, it was what he said" (p. 102).

Jews don't agree on just who qualifies to be included in a minyan. Orthodox Jews, who used to require (and maybe still do) women to sit apart from men at services, do not count women for a minyan, though some, maybe most, Conservative Jews do. Orthodox and Conservative Jews do not consider people whose father was Jewish but whose mother was not Jewish to be officially Jewish, so they presumably would not include them in a minyan. I, as is probably clear by now, am not especially observant or big on Jewish ritual, so I'm ready to claim that even with the varied group of Guilford faculty I have identified as Jewish we have enough for a hypothetical Zoom minyan. Sheridan Simon, Jackie Ludel, and Sam Schuman are no longer alive (as my mother would say, her knee jerking slightly upward, "may they rest in peace"), but if we were actually to do such a Zoom minyan, we would have people Zooming in who now live in and around Greensboro, but also some from California, Canada, and Israel.

My wife and I do religiously practice one Jewish ritual: on the anniversaries of the deaths of family members and other loved ones, we light yahrzeit candles, those little candles in a glass that burn for about 24 hours that you can find in the grocery store near the matzah and gefilte fish. We light these candles on the evenings before these loved ones had died, and then, walking by the candle as we go about our daily lives for the next day or so, we are reminded of them. We do this not only for our four parents, but for Ed Burrows, a Guilford faculty member we were close with, for Bob Kingman, a college friend, and for the many dogs who have been our daily companions over the years. (And my mother thought I was not observant!).

The Jewish faculty at Guilford are a varied lot, with some, like Adele Wayman, having left their childhood Judaism either completely behind or maintain it in some mixture with other spiritual traditions; some, like me, still Jewish but unaffiliated and unobservant; some still Jewish and observant; and some, like the Malinos, observant and affiliated with one of the Greensboro congregations. Two had parents who survived the Holocaust, one grew up in a family that was a member of an Orthodox synagogue, a few have been to Israel many times, and one is a rabbi, the son of a rabbi, and the father of a rabbi.[16]

16. Here are the names, departments, and years they have taught at Guilford: Richie Zweigenhaft, Psychology, 1974-2020; Sheridan Simon, Physics, 1974-1994; Jackie Ludel, Biology and Psychology, 1976-1996; Jonathan Malino, Philosophy, 1976-2015; Roy Nydorf, Art, 1978-2018; Sarah Malino, History, 1979-2013; Steve Shapiro, Physics, 1995-2016; Julie Burke, Education Studies, 2004-2020; Adam Golub, Education Studies, 2004-2007; Bob Malekoff, Sports Studies, 2005-2014; Sarah Estow, Psychology, 2006-2020; David Hammond, Theatre Studies, 2007-2017; Rachel Riskind, Psychology, 2013-2020; Karen Spira, 2013-2020. There may have been others I am unaware of, and when I double-checked to confirm that one faculty member was Jewish, that person told me that they were, but asked that I not include their name in any publication (they did not explain why).

In November, 2020, someone who read an early edition of the book asked me if Rudy Behar, who taught English from 1968–1987, was Jewish. I knew Rudy and had no inkling that he was Jewish (he did not register on my Jewdar). He died in January, 2020, but I now have learned that his parents were both Jewish. His mother died when he was young and his father was unable to care for him. He was brought up in a series of foster homes, and at one point was in a Jewish orphanage. He was married in a Jewish ceremony, but was not a practicing Jew and he considered himself an atheist. It is likely that he also considered himself to be a Jew.

2 *The Palestinians on the Faculty*

AS I HAVE NOTED, back in 1974, under Grimsley Hobbs and Bruce Stewart's leadership, Guilford began to conduct national, rather than regional searches, and this resulted in faculty coming to Guilford from all around the country, with degrees from schools in California (me, from UCSC, others from UCLA and some from Stanford), from schools in the Midwest (such as the University of Chicago), and schools throughout New England (including Harvard, Yale, and Princeton, to name the elite trinity). The faculty in 1974 was, it seemed to me, exceptionally good when it came to pedagogy and caring about their students, but not many had published very much, and many had not published at all.

Some of the searches the college conducted were not just national but international. Or, to put it more accurately, the college at times hired people who were from all over the world, even if they did not come to Guilford directly from the countries of their birth. Over the years, I have had colleagues from Panama, Russia, Japan, New Zealand,

Canada, Spain, China, and, importantly for this narrative, two Palestinians.[1]

The first of the two Palestinians hired by Guilford was Mohammed Abu-Nimer. After earning both a B.A. and an M.A. from Hebrew University, in 1993 he completed his doctoral dissertation at George Mason University—the title of his dissertation was "Conflict Resolution Between Arabs and Jews in Israel." He and his wife (also a Palestinian, also working on a Ph.D. degree) wanted to stay in the USA, and so he entered the academic job market. An article in *Peacebuilder*, published by the Center for Justice and Peacebuilding, recounted his experience in the following way:

> His desire to work in this country made sense at the time. His wife Ilham, also born in a Palestinian town in Israel, was working on a PhD in early childhood education, and they had a young son (later joined by a daughter) they wanted to raise in the United States.
>
> Abu-Nimer was rejected 176 times.
>
> "Nobody wanted to take a fresh graduate in conflict resolution from the Middle East," Abu-Nimer recalled in a November 2014 interview with *Peacebuilder*, adding that conflict resolution was just beginning to be recognized as a field of study.
>
> The 177th application he filed—with Guilford, a small Quaker-rooted college in North Carolina—finally yielded a job offer. Vernie Davis, then an anthropology professor who also taught on peace and conflict topics,

1. Here and throughout I have focused on full-time tenure-track positions because they indicate a long-term commitment on the part of the college. Another Palestinian, Salem Ajluni, taught for two years in a full-time contingent position in the Economics department in the late 1980s.

hired Abu-Nimer in 1993-94 to teach about religion as a source of both conflict and peace.[2]

So, Mohammed came to Guilford, joined the Sociology/ Anthropology Department and became the Coordinator of the Peace and Conflict Studies program and the Director of the Conflict Resolution Resource Center. He stayed for only four years before he left for a job at American University (now a tenured Full Professor, he has written, coauthored or edited eleven books). During his years at Guilford, he taught courses in sociology, he ran programs on conflict resolution and mediation, he participated on panels, and he invited speakers to the campus.

Mohammed was not working alone in his efforts to provide a perspective on the Middle East that differed from the one that was issued from the pulpits of the synagogue and the temple. Not only was Max Carter, the campus minister, participating in programs on campus and in the community and leading groups to Israel and Palestine (Max was later to lead three of these trips with Jonathan Malino), but Joe Groves, a professor in the Religious Studies department, also was teaching courses about the Middle East. An activist, Joe worked on many social justice issues. When Joe (neither a Palestinian, nor a Quaker, nor Jewish) left Guilford in 2001, after having taught at the college for 22 years, he moved to Washington, D.C., where he worked first for the Fellowship of Reconciliation (FOR), and then he became the leader of what was the FOR's new Israel/Palestine program, Interfaith Peace-Builders (which then became an independent non-profit, separate from the

2. Lofton, Bonnie Price. 2001. "AU's Peace Institute 2001: Practice, Scholarship, and Development," *Peacebuilder*, Issue 2014-2015. https:// emu.edu/now/peacebuilder/2015/07/aus-peace-institute-2001- practice-scholarship-and-development/

Fellowship). In April 2001, when students and alumni gathered at a dinner to honor Joe, according to an article in the student newspaper, *The Guilfordian*, Joe explained that "This move [to D.C.] gives me a chance to cause a lot more trouble. It will give me a chance to have a deeper and more active level in political struggles and social justice."[3]

In 2008, the college hired Amal Khoury to teach in the Peace and Conflict Studies program (by this time it had become one of the interdisciplinary majors at the college). Born in Beirut, Amal described herself to me in an email in the following way: "I am Lebanese, not Palestinian. My mom, however, was Palestinian-Lebanese." Amal did undergraduate work at American University in Beirut, and she subsequently received her Ph.D. at American University (in Washington, D.C.), where her dissertation advisor was Mohammed Abu-Nimer. She left Guilford in 2014 for a position at the University of North Carolina, Charlotte.

In 2008, the college also hired Diya Abdo to join the English department. Diya is a Palestinian who was born and raised in Jordan. How's that? Born and raised in Jordan but a Palestinian? Diya's grandparents left Palestine for Jordan in 1967. Although they lived for many decades in Jordan, they and Diya consider themselves Palestinians (there are more than 2 million people registered as Palestinian refugees in Jordan, and more who are of Palestinian origin).[4] In 2015, Diya started a program

3. Eppsteiner, Ty. 2001. "A Farewell to Joe Groves," *The Guilfordian*, April 13, https://www.guilfordian.com/archives/2001/04/13/a-farewell-to-joe-groves/

4. When I moved 3,000 miles from Santa Cruz, CA, to Greensboro, NC, it was something of a culture shock, but nothing compared to the move Diya Abdo made, 6,000 miles, from Jordan to Greensboro. See Abdo, Diya. 2015. "Sayf," in *27 Views of Greensboro: The Gate City in Prose and Poetry*. Hillsborough, NC: Eno Publishers, pp. 47-53.

called Every Campus a Refuge (ECAR). Partnering with the Greensboro office of Church World Services, the program provides newly arrived immigrants with temporary housing on the campus, food, utilities, Wi-Fi, and support from the campus community, until they can resettle successfully in Greensboro. The program has spread to many other campuses and has been recognized by both the White House and the United Nations. As of early 2020, Guilford's program had hosted 52 families, and the college had created an interdisciplinary minor called "Every Campus a Refuge."

So with Max Carter, who came to Guilford in 1990, and who had decades of contacts with people he first met in Ramallah in the early 1970s, Mohammed Abu-Nimer, who taught at the college in the 1990s, Joe Groves, whose time at Guilford spanned the 1980s and 1990s, and some years later, Amal Khoury, at the college from 2008–2014, Diya Abdo, at the college from 2008–2020, not to mention the critiques of Israel that Jonathan Malino contributed to the mix from the time he was hired in 1976 until he retired in 2015, all of them willing to speak their minds, knowledge about Palestine and attitudes about Israel were changing on campus—and I should add, on other campuses around the country. The rosy image that some of us grew up with, as we raised money to plant trees in Israel— that Israel was a land of milk and honey, a land that Jews had converted from a barren desert, somehow without people, into a productive oasis that was, moreover, the only democracy in the Middle East—needed readjustment. Although I never sensed a major conflict between the Jews and the Quakers on campus, there was a growing divide between the Greensboro Jewish community and the college, and by 2015 there were sharp divisions within the small Jewish student community on campus.

3   *Jews and Politics*

JEWS TEND TO BE liberal in their voting patterns. This is apparent in the ways they have voted in Presidential elections. As can be seen in Appendix 1, which shows how Jews have voted in each presidential election since 1916, over that 100-year period American Jews have consistently voted for Democrats. To use the last two elections as examples, 69% of the Jewish vote went to Obama in 2012, compared to only 51% of the national vote, and 71% of the Jewish vote went to Hillary Clinton in 2016 compared to only 48% of the national vote. Looking a bit further back, in 1960, 82% voted for Kennedy over Nixon, and in 1964, 90% voted for Johnson over Goldwater. As Appendix 1 shows, in every election since 1916 a higher percentage of Jews voted for the Democratic candidate than for the Republican candidate. Moreover, in all of these elections the percentage of Jews who voted for the Democratic candidates exceeded the percentage of national voters who went for the Democratic candidate.

Jews not only have been consistently liberal in their voting patterns, they also have been disproportionately represented among social justice activists. As just one of many examples I could give, consider this: in the Mississippi Freedom Summer in 1964, when about 3 percent of the American population was Jewish, not only were two of the three freedom riders who were murdered by Klansmen Jewish (Michael Schwerner and Andrew Goodman—the other, James Chaney, was black), but at least half of the hundreds of young people who participated in the freedom summer were Jewish.[1]

I don't have comparable data for how Quakers voted from 1916 through 2016, but, given the high level of commitment that many Quakers displayed during the abolitionist movement, and more recently, in the civil rights movement, and in the anti-war movement during the Vietnam years, it is clear that some Quakers have been at the forefront on issues related to race relations, peace, and social justice. I have found only one empirical study that looked at Quaker voting patterns, and that was in the 2008 presidential race. In that online study of a small sample of 181 Quaker voters, Wess Daniels found that 83% voted for Obama over McCain (a figure quite close to the 78% of the national Jewish sample that voted for Obama that year).[2] However, Max Carter assures me that many Quakers, including most of his Midwest family, vote Republican, and that many even voted for Trump, so I am hesitant to generalize about Quaker voting patterns nationally or even in North Carolina. One thing I learned when I came to Guilford College is that not all Quakers are like those liberal Philadelphia Quakers whom

1. Dreier, Peter. 2020."Martin Luther King Jr., the Civil Rights Movement, and American Jews," *Los Angeles Review of Books*, January 18. https://lareviewofbooks.org/article/martin-luther-king-jr-the-civil-rights-movement-and-american-jews/; see, also, Klatch, Rebecca E. 1999. *A Generation Divided: The New Left, the New Right, and the 1960s* (University of California Press), p. 10 and p. 39.

2. Daniels, Wess. 2008. "Quaker Voting Poll, 2008." https://www.slideshare.net/cwdaniels/quaker-voting-presentation

I worked with in the late 1960s during the anti-war movement, and that many Quakers are both evangelical and politically conservative. In fact, Quaker writer and activist Chuck Fager reports that 80% of the Quakers in America are evangelical, that he is convinced that in 2008 and 2012 the North Carolina evangelical Quakers voted heavily against Obama, and that in 2016 they voted heavily for Trump.[3] If I had known more about these evangelical Quakers (or even that they existed!) when I entered the job market, back in the fall of 1973, I might not have applied for the job at Guilford. Fortunately for me, the Quakers at Guilford, for the most part, have not been from that 80%—they more likely have been progressives who went to schools like George School, Westtown, or Earlham, and more likely to have supported Obama in 2008 and 2012 and Hillary Clinton in 2016.

There was a notable decline in Jewish support for the Democratic nominee running for President in 1980: whereas 71% of the Jewish vote went for Carter in 1976 when he ran against Gerald Ford, four years later when Carter ran again Ronald Reagan he received only 45% of the Jewish vote (Reagan received 39% of the Jewish vote). What happened?

What happened was Israel and Palestine. In the late 1970s, many Jews came to see Carter as insufficiently supportive of Israel, and too accommodating to the Palestinians. His efforts to bring peace to the Middle East, and to achieve a two-state solution, did lead to the Camp David Accords in 1978, two signed agreements between Israeli Prime Minister Menachem Begin and Egyptian Anwar Sadat that followed twelve days of secret negotiations coordinated by Carter and his

3. Fager, Chuck. 2020. "A Catholic Reckoning? How About an Evangelical Quaker Reckoning?" *A Friendly Letter*, April 28. https://afriendlyletter.com/a-catholic-reckoning-how-about-an-evangelical-quaker-reckoning/#more-15941

administration. The second agreement led months later to the Egypt-Israel Peace Treaty, and Begin and Sadat were awarded the Nobel Prize for Peace in 1978.

Despite the success of the Camp David Accords, Carter was seen by many American Jews as too critical of Israel, and too supportive of the Palestinians. These perceptions were exacerbated when it was revealed in August 1979, that Andrew Young, Carter's Ambassador to the United Nations (the first African American to hold that position), in an attempt to delay a UN report calling for the creation of a Palestinian state, had met with the UN representative of the Palestinian Liberation Organization (PLO) at the home of the Kuwaiti Ambassador to the UN. US officials were not supposed to talk with representatives of the PLO because the organization had not recognized Israel's right to exist, and when his secret meeting with the representative of the PLO was exposed, Young was forced to resign.[4] Carter's campaign for the presidency in 1980

4. In an interview 14 years later, Young had this to say: "There was never any question in my mind that I was on the side of peace. In Congress, I had a 100% voting record in support of Israel. The climate here was irrational and you couldn't get any reasonable discussion and hope to be reelected, so the closer Jimmy Carter got to (the 1980) election, the less you could talk about it. Unfortunately, the Jewish community in America tended to identify with the right-wing element in Israeli politics.... My positions on Israel were formulated out of the original Israeli vision of coexistence with Palestinians." Scheer, Robert. 1993. "Lessons from a Missed Opportunity: Eyewitness: Andrew Young," *Los Angeles Times*, September 12. https://www.latimes.com/archives/la-xpm-1993-09-12-op-34888-story.html

Similarly, Carter's commitment to a two-state solution did not wane, nor did his willingness to criticize Israel. See Carter, Jimmy. 2016. "American Must Recognize Palestine," *New York Times*, Nov. 29, A27.

In his 2018 book, *President Carter: The White House Years*, Stuart Eisenstadt (Atlanta-born, educated at UNC and then the Harvard also saw a decline in contributions from major Jewish donors. Just as McGovern in 1972 lost the support of many Jewish contributors when he gave what was seen as the wrong answer in response to a question about Israel at a meeting with major Jewish fund raisers in New York City, so, too, did Carter lose financial support from Jewish donors in 1980.[5]

Jimmy Carter was, and is, a serious Christian, not a Quaker, but his views on the Middle East were very much influenced by a Quaker who was quite well known on the Guilford College campus. Landrum Bolling, trained as a political scientist and a convinced Quaker (raised as a Baptist, he married a Quaker, and soon became a Quaker himself), was the President of Earlham College from 1958 to 1973. In 1968, after a three-week visit

Law School, and Carter's Chief Domestic Policy Advisor during his presidency), a strong supporter of Israel, argues that Carter has been seriously underrated as a president. See Baker, Peter. 2018. "Was Jimmy Carter the Most Underrated President in History?" *New York Times*, June 5. https://www.nytimes.com/2018/06/05/books/review/president-carter-stuart-eizenstat.html

5. Domhoff, G. William. 1990. *The Power Elite and the State: How Policy is Made in America*, New York: Aldine de Gruyter, p. 249. In his excellent book, *Jews and American Politics*, Stephen Isaacs explains what happened when McGovern was asked about his position on Israel: "The only hope for a just and permanent settlement in the Middle East, McGovern answered…was not an imposed peace, but a negotiated one, worked out in a world forum like the United Nations. With that answer, McGovern blew most of the traditional big money from Jews in 1972….According to one man present, McGovern mentioning the United Nations 'was like waving a red flag in front of a bull'" (p. 4).

As can be seen in Appendix 1, 81% of the Jewish vote went to Humphrey in 1968, but that figure dropped to 65% for McGovern in 1972; it climbed back to 71% for Carter in 1976 but, as I have noted, it dropped all the way to 45% in 1980.

to the Middle East, Bolling wrote the following passage in an article for the *Friends Journal: Quaker Thought and Life Today*:

"What the Israelis really want," several prominent West Bank Arabs told me, "is for us to help them set up a Quisling government. They don't want the continued headaches of trying to rule us through an army of occupation, but we don't intend to accept the Nazi pattern, even if it is now proposed by Jews." Nothing about their relations with the Arabs infuriates the Israelis so much as to have their actions compared with those of the Nazis, yet there have been enough cases of Israeli military brutality to give the Arabs a sense of justification for their hatred and an increasing admiration for the guerilla fighters of the Al-Fatah. The longer acts of terror and counter-terror continue the more difficult it will be to make peace.[6]

Two years later, based on the work of an international task force that studied Israeli-Palestinian-Arab conflicts in the aftermath of the Six-Day War of 1967, Bolling expanded on that brief *Friends Journal* article and wrote a book titled *Search for Peace in the Middle East*, published by the American Friends Service Committee. The book was widely read and controversial. According to Thomas Hamm, a Professor of History and the curator of the Quaker collection at Earlham College, "Some saw it as an even-handed but compassionate analysis of the region's problems, with its clear sympathies for the plight of Palestinians. Others attacked it as unduly critical of Israel and unrealistic in its call for Israeli withdrawal from

6. Bolling, Landrum R. 1968. "What Chance for Peace in the Middle East," *Friends Journal: Quaker Thought and Life Today*, September 1, p. 433.

occupied lands."[7] Either way, it helped inspire the commitment that many have come to hold for a two-state solution. When he stepped down as President at Earlham in 1973, Bolling became involved in international diplomacy for several presidential administrations. More specifically, and especially relevant here, he served in the late 1970s as a liaison between the Carter administration and the Palestinian Liberation Organization (PLO). In a tribute when Bolling turned 100, Jimmy Carter wrote the following: "Knowing of his personal acquaintance with Israeli and Arab leaders and his experience in the region, I turned to him for advice and assistance while negotiating the Camp David Accords while I was president." Four years later, when Bolling died at 104, Carter (age 94) told the family in a condolence call, "Landrum was one of my heroes."[8]

7. Bolling, Landrum R. 1970. *Search for Peace in the Middle East.* Philadelphia, PA: American Friends Service Committee; Hamm, Thomas. "Landrum Bolling: Advocate for Peace," Earlham College, https://earlham.edu/media/2940505/Landrum-Bolling-obituary. pdf. The book was also severely criticized by some Arabs because it recognized Israel and called for a two-state solution.

8. Barnes, Bart. 2018. "Landrum Bolling, college president, peace activist and presidential go-between dies at 104," *Washington Post*, January 30; https://www.washingtonpost.com/local/obituaries/landrum-bolling-college-president-peace-activist-and-presidential-go-between-dies-at-104/2018/01/30/2f0a1060-053a-11e8-8777-2a059f168dd2_story.html

4   After Jimmy Carter: The 1980s

IT WAS IN THIS national context (Carter having lost substantial support in the Jewish community nationally and Reagan having been elected in 1980), and in the local context (an increasingly diversified faculty at Guilford which included those who were outspoken in their criticisms of Israel) that two key events took place on the Guilford campus.

The first event was a panel about the Middle East in Sternberger Auditorium in the fall of 1982, not long after the Israeli invasion of Lebanon in June 1982 (known in Lebanon as "the invasion," it is called "the Lebanon War" or the "the First Lebanon War" in Israel). The invasion, or the war, had generated widespread criticism of Israel, and the leaders in the local community were under increasing pressure to defend Israel. The leadership at Temple Emanuel agreed to co-sponsor a panel on Israel and Palestine on the Guilford College campus (they had been asked to sponsor Israel-Palestine events previously, but had refused to do so). A group of those planning the event met to establish who would be on the panel, and the ground rules. Although those from Guilford lobbied to include a panelist from the

Greensboro Palestinian community, that was a red line for those at the temple. The Guilford faculty reluctantly agreed that there would be no Palestinians on the panel.

The panel was moderated by Bruce Stewart (then the Assistant to the President). The participants were two Guilford faculty members, Jonathan Malino and Joe Groves, and two faculty members from nearby schools, Elias Abu-Saba, a Lebanese professor of Engineering at North Carolina A&T, and Svi Shapiro, Jewish, and a professor of Education and Cultural Studies at UNCG. There were hundreds of people in attendance, and the atmosphere was tense. As had been established in the ground rules, Bruce allowed the audience to submit only written questions, but then a Palestinian in the audience rose to complain, saying that he wanted to ask a question, noting that there were no Palestinians on the panel. In the face of this challenge, and in this tense atmosphere, those on the panel, including Bruce, hastily conferred and decided to allow the Palestinian five minutes to present his views. He did, and the audience received his comments respectfully.

There were, however, some tense discussions immediately afterwards, and those at the temple, especially Arnold Task, the rabbi, felt that allowing the Palestinian to speak was a betrayal of the agreement that had been made. Moreover, because the two Jews on the panel, Jonathan Malino and Svi Shapiro, were quite critical of Israel, as were Joe Groves and Elias Abu-Saba, many in the audience from the Jewish community felt the panel had been one-sided and anti-Israel.

In thinking back on this event, Joe Groves, now retired and living in Chapel Hill, drew these conclusions:

> It was reasonable for them to be upset—we broke the ground rules that we had agreed to. I think we did the right thing in the moment, but I understand their sense of betrayal.

A positive outcome of the panel was a quiet but sustained Jewish-Palestinian dialogue. After the panel some Jewish audience members talked with the Palestinian and said they wanted to continue the conversation. Jonathan and (I think) Mark Shapiro organized an evening of conversation that included some members of the Jewish community, some Greensboro Palestinians, me, and Elias. I think we met at Mark's house. (The vast majority of the Greensboro Palestinian community were Christians from Ramallah. They were familiar with Quakers because of the Ramallah Friends School.) The conversations happened every couple of months for two or three years. They were respectful, warm, and honest. A lot of it was about Israel and Palestine, but also a lot about being a Jew or an Arab, and about family and friendship.[1]

A second event took place on campus, later in that decade, that served to reinforce what had become fairly widespread perceptions in the local Jewish community that some, maybe many, on the Guilford campus were critical of Israel. This event took place in 1989, during the First Intifada, when, again, there was widespread criticism of Israel both nationally and locally (and internationally for that matter). Arnold Task had left the temple for a congregation in Louisiana, a new rabbi, Rick Harkavy, had arrived, and he and the temple leadership again agreed to co-sponsor an event on the Guilford College campus. This time, there was to be a speaker—Landrum Bolling—

1. These recollections are from an email I received from Joe Groves, April 28, 2020. Jonathan Malino concurred with Joe's recollections, with one slight difference: he recalls that Bruce Stewart handled the written questions and participated in the decision to allow the Palestinian to speak but was not the moderator.

followed by a panel that consisted of Jonathan Malino (still Jewish, still a rabbi), Joe Groves (still not Jewish, not Quaker, not a Palestinian), the new rabbi, and a Palestinian who was a graduate student at N.C. A & T. This was, as far as those of us trying to reconstruct this event can tell, the first time a Greensboro rabbi appeared on a panel with a Palestinian, and it did not go well. Joe Groves recalls that the rabbi was ineffective and hostile:

> Rather than present an Israeli perspective on the conflict or even address what Landrum said, he spent most of his time criticizing Guilford for having the event and implying that we were anti-Semitic. When I spoke with him afterwards and objected to what he said, he basically replied, "What do you expect me to say—I can't counter *Landrum Bolling*."

This event only added to the negative image many in the local Jewish community had of Guilford. Within a few years, Rabbi Harkavy was gone (perhaps his willingness to participate in this event or his ineffectiveness contributed to his departure). He was followed by an interim rabbi, and then, in 1995 the temple hired a new rabbi, Fred Guttman. "When Fred Guttman arrived," Joe recalled, "he made it clear that he was going to be a strong advocate for Israel and filled that role well. During the 1990s…Guttman contested any inclusion of the Israeli-Palestinian conflict in any social justice initiative, particularly within the African-American community."

5 Into the 1990s

THERE WERE NO NEW Jewish faculty added to the tenure track ranks during the 1980s and 1990s, unless my Jewdar has failed me and I am missing some people. There always have been Quakers on the faculty, but not very many—during the time I have been at the college I doubt that card-carrying Quakers were ever more than 10-15% of the faculty, if that.[1] And, as I have noted, the college hired the first of two Palestinians in

1. Although the percentage of the faculty who have been Quakers has been relatively low, many have been, as the Quakes say, "weighty," and they have been central to keeping the spirit of Quakerism alive on the campus, including at the monthly faculty meetings. During the 1980s and 1990s these included Rex Adelberger (Physics), David Barnhill (Religious Studies), Ted Benfey (Chemistry), Vernie Davis (Sociology/Anthropology), Thom Espinola (Physics), Rudy Gordh (Math), Cyril Harvey (Geology), Jim Hood (English), Cyrus Johnson (Sociology/Anthropology), Raymond Johnson (Accounting), Beth Keiser (English), Mel Keiser (Religion), Tim Lindeman (Music), Dave MacInnes (Chemistry), Pete Moore (Religious Studies), Elwood Parker (Math), Gwen Reddick (Ed Studies), Deborah Roose (Education Studies), Don Smith (Physics), and Paul Zopf (Sociology/Anthropology).

1993, Mohammed Abu-Nimer (another, Diya Abdo, was hired in 2008).[2]

What about students? For many years, about 4-5% of the traditional-age students were Quaker, so in an entering class of 300 students, maybe there were 15 Quakers, and about 60 or so in all four classes. When the Quaker Leadership Scholars Program (QLSP) was established in 1992, a goal was set to increase the number of Quaker students on campus, and this in fact happened. An admissions report for 2007–2016 reveals that the number of Quaker students rose to 118 (9%) in 2008 but declined steadily over the next nine years—there were only 43 (4%) in 2017.[3]

And Jewish students? It is harder to know how many Jewish students there were as the admissions reports typically did not break down the entering classes by religion (other than Quakers). Moreover, there were likely many students over the years with one Jewish parent, who may or may not have identified as Jewish (or, for that matter, with two Jewish parents but who did not identify as Jewish). Based on Jonathan Malino's role as advisor to Hillel for many years, and my role as advisor

2. As noted in Footnote #1 of Chapter 2, another Palestinian, Salem Ajluni, taught for two years in a full-time contingent position in the Economics department in the late 1980s.

3. The overall enrollment at the college declined during those years but not as dramatically as the decline in the number of Quakers; https://www.guilford.edu/sites/default/files/2018-08/Data%20 Digest%202017-2018.pdf .

Notably, the number of Quakers on the faculty and staff also have declined dramatically. Whereas there were at least 30 Quakers on the faculty and staff throughout most of the 1980s and 1990s, by the beginning of the 2019-2020 academic year there were fewer than 10. As of the spring of 2020, there were only four Quaker faculty holding tenure-track positions: Thom Espinola (Physics), Jim Hood (English), Dani Moran (Math) and Don Smith (Physics).

for a few years when Jonathan was not around, we estimate that in a typical year in the 1980s and 1990s there were 30-40 Jewish students on campus.

And what about Palestinian students? From 1946-1948, former Religious Studies professor Pete Moore, who grew up in the Revolution Mills community in Greensboro (his father worked for Cone Mills), and his wife Lucretia spent two years doing Friends mission work at the Ramallah Friends School, the same school where Max Carter was to work as a conscientious objector in the early 1970s. Just as a decade later he recruited Bruce Stewart to come to Guilford from Massachusetts (a Quaker school in North Carolina? "Where's that, and what's a Quaker?"), while in Ramallah Pete recruited some Palestinian students to come to Guilford from the Ramallah Friends School. By 1990, when Pete organized a reunion of Palestinian Guilford alumni, he was able to get nine or ten of them to show up. Throughout the 1980s and 1990s, however, there were few or no Palestinian students on campus. In 1999 Don McNemar, Guilford's President from 1996 through 2002,[4] was

4. Don McNemar, Guilford's seventh president, was, like all who served in that office before him, a Quaker. And, like every president who preceded him except for Lewis Lyndon Hobbs, he had Earlham connections. Thomas Newlin, Guilford's second president, graduated from Earlham. Raymond Binford, Guilford's third president, was an undergraduate at Earlham, and subsequently taught biology there. Clyde Milner, Guilford's fourth president, taught at Earlham, as did Grimsley Hobbs, Guilford's fifth president. Bill Rogers, Guilford's sixth president, came to Guilford from a faculty position at Harvard, but he previously taught at Earlham. McNemar, Guilford's seventh president, was an undergraduate at Earlham. The next two presidents, Kent Chabotar and Jane Fernandes, had no Earlham connections, and neither was a Quaker when hired, though after she arrived Fernandes and her husband became members of one of the local Quaker meetings (Friendship Friends).

able to designate some existing scholarship money to create what were called the Ramallah Scholarships. Because of those scholarships, each year for about four years, there were 2-3 Palestinian students arriving (some with support from this scholarship, others with other sources of support). However, the college was unable to raise enough money to establish an endowed fund to pay for these scholarships, and the amount of support was at first reduced, and then, during one of Guilford's many budget crunches, the Ramallah Scholarships were eliminated. The number of Palestinian students on campus declined. Still, for several years early in this 21st century, the period I plan to focus on momentarily, there were Palestinian students on campus, and there was an increasing number of Palestinian alumni.

6 *The Emergence of Boycott, Divest, and Sanctions (BDS) in 2005, and Its Effects on Academe, Including Guilford*

IN 2005, AT ABOUT the same time that Guilford College sponsored a two-day colloquium titled "Voices from Palestine and Israel: 'Living for Peace' in a Holy Land," funded by the Guilford Initiative on Faith and Practice, and by a grant from the Lilly Foundation (see Appendix 2), a group of Palestinians formed the Boycott, Divest, and Sanctions (BDS) movement. Modeled after the boycott of South Africa that took place during that country's apartheid regime, over the next decade BDS gradually gained both supporters and detractors. Among the supporters were many notable figures with liberal or leftist leanings, including Desmond Tutu, Angela Davis, Naomi Klein, and Stephen Hawking. Tutu, for example, had this to say: "In South Africa, we could not have achieved our democracy without the help of people around the world, who through the use of non-violent means, such as boycotts and divestment, encouraged their governments and other corporate actors to reverse decades-long support for the apartheid regime." [1]

1. Tutu, Desmond. 2014. "My Plea to the People of Israel: Liberate Yourselves by Liberating Palestine". *Haaretz*, August 14.

Some prominent leftists, however, were among the most vociferous detractors, including Cary Nelson, Professor of English and the President of the American Association of University Professors (AAUP) from 2006 through 2012. Nelson wrote a 700-page book titled *Israel Denial: Anti-Zionism, Anti-Semitism, & the Faculty Campaign Against the Jewish State*. In Nelson's view, colleges and universities have been fertile grounds for the BDS movement "because faculty and students can become passionate about justice, sometimes without adequate knowledge about the facts and consequences. ... [U]niversities also offer the potential for small numbers of BDS activists to leverage institutional status and reputation for a more significant cultural and political impact." [2]

The movement gathered momentum in the USA and around the world, especially on college campuses and in professional academic associations. Students organized to try to persuade their boards of trustees to divest from Israel, or to try to persuade their dining halls not to order hummus from Israel. After the 2018 mid-term election, in which a group of four Democratic women of color were elected, two of whom came out clearly in support of the BDS movement, the U. S. House of Representatives passed a resolution condemning it. Three writers for the *New York Times* concluded that the considerable turmoil on campuses and at meetings of faculty associations had not accomplished much: "Actual accomplishments have been minimal: a few dozen resolutions in university student assemblies; a handful of decisions by law-enforcement agencies to stop training with the Israeli military; votes by two faculty groups last year—the Association

2. Nelson, Cary, and Gabriel Brahm. 2015. *The Case Against Academic Boycotts of Israel, MLA Members for Scholars Rights*, p., 13. See also, Nelson, Cary. 2019. *Israel Denial: Anti-Zionism, Anti-Semitism, & the Faculty Campaign Against the Jewish State*. Bloomington, IN: Indiana University Press.

for Asian American Studies and the larger American Studies Association — for limited boycotts of Israeli academia." Still, the article went on to note, despite these limited accomplishments, and despite the House resolution (and laws in at least 26 states barring contracts with companies that endorse BDS), surveys indicated that between 20% and 40% of Americans supported the idea of boycotting Israel.[3]

3. Halbfinger, David, Michael Wines, and Steven Erlanger. 2019. "A Look at the International Drive to Boycott Israel," *New York Times*, July 28, Section A, p. 8.

7 *Hillel, Open Hillel, and Chavurah*

A SPIN-OFF ISSUE, related to the BDS movement, arose after the International Hillel organization published standards of partnership guidelines which stated that "Hillel will not partner with, house, or host organizations, groups, or speakers that as a matter of policy or practice….support boycott of, divestment from, or sanctions against the State of Israel." This rankled some Hillel students who wanted their organizations to be able to continue to sponsor, or at least be co-hosts of, panels that included speakers with opposing viewpoints when it came to boycotts, divestment and sanctions. This led to the emergence of a Hillel-alternative called Open Hillel, first at Harvard in 2012, at Swarthmore in 2013, at Vassar in 2014, and at Wesleyan also in 2014. The mission statement for Open Hillel was the following:

> We seek to change the "standards for partnership" in Hillel International's guidelines, which exclude certain groups from Hillel based on their political views on Israel. In addition, we encourage local campus Hillels

to adopt policies that are more open and inclusive than Hillel International's, and that allow for free discourse on all subjects within the Hillel community.

In April 2014, after some Guilford students attended an Open Hillel conference held at Harvard, Guilford's Hillel decided to join Harvard, Swarthmore, Vassar, and Wesleyan by becoming an Open Hillel group. Nicole Zelniker, the vice-president of Guilford's Hillel group, wrote the following press release:

> Tonight, Guilford College Hillel has taken a huge step in practicing our core values of community, equality, integrity and diversity: we have declared ourselves to be an open Hillel. Consistent with the beliefs that drew us to Guilford, we are striving to build an inclusive and accessible Jewish community on our campus.
>
> At Guilford's Hillel, we have a wide range of Jewish voices. We have Zionists, anti-Zionists and everything in between. On our campus, it is an imperative that Hillel be a place that is for all Jewish students, irrespective of their political ideology. As an open Hillel, we believe that Jewish students should be supported in expressing their Jewish identity and values in the way that is most meaningful to them.
>
> As of now, Hillel International's Standards of Partnership state that an organization bearing the name Hillel cannot partner with groups supporting Boycott, Divestment and Sanctions and that Hillel must support Israel. If we want to ensure that all students feel welcome and supported in the one Jewish organization at Guilford, it is crucial that inclusiveness be the paramount value of our community. As an open Hillel we can embrace the political diversity of

our community and will use our differences to promote our personal, intellectual and Jewish growth.

To be an open Hillel is to welcome all perspectives on Israel-Palestine. By declaring ourselves open, we affirm our organization to be an accepting place for all on Guilford's campus.

The press release generated national attention, and it also generated considerable discussion on campus and in the local Jewish community. As more Jewish students at Guilford became aware of the change from Hillel to Open Hillel, and what it meant, they debated whether to be a Hillel group, to remain with Open Hillel, or to use another designation. Almost a year later, perhaps influenced also by the fact that International Hillel had threated to sue both the Guilford Open Hillel and the Swarthmore Open Hillel for trademark violation, the group decided to change its name once again, this time to Chavurah. In an article titled "How Guilford Hillel Became Guilford Chavurah," written for a publication titled *New Voices*, Nicole Zelniker wrote the following:

At 8:17 a.m. on a rainy Thursday morning, a group of nine Jewish students at Guilford College decided to make a change.

Rather than continuing to label themselves as a Hillel, the students decided to dub themselves Guilford Chavurah, meaning "group of friends" in Hebrew.

At first, students saw joining Open Hillel, a student-led campaign to pressure Hillel International to divorce itself from its standards of partnership, as a potential way to make more students feel welcome. This became a particularly attractive option when students decided to host an Open Hillel-sponsored national campus tour featuring Jewish Civil Rights veterans and strident critics of Israel Dorothy Zellner, Ira Grupper, and Larry Rubin.

Many students do feel safe in Hillel, particularly Zionist Jews. For this reason, many Guilford students opposed the idea of "opening" their Hillel. "Hillel for me is a religious organization, an organization that celebrates Jewish life," said senior Josh Weil. "Open Hillel, in my eyes, is political."

Senior Sara Minsky disagrees. "No matter your political ideologies, students should be able to come to Hillel and feel like they should be able to talk about these issues," she said.

In light of irreconcilable views on Zionism within the community, Guilford's Jewish students felt the group needed to focus on club structure and Jewish culture rather than politics.

"We're not sure where we are right now, so we decided not to sponsor any political based events," said sophomore and treasurer of Guilford Chavurah Lizzie Hart.

In restructuring their community, many students are taking a comment Zellner made on the panel about the need to discuss the matter with everyone in the community as a guiding principle through the transition. In order to foster a more inclusive discussion, Guilford Chavurah put off many major decisions about the club's future until next fall, when the next class of students will arrive.[1]

1. Zelniker, Nicole. 2015. "How Guilford Hillel Became Guilford Chavurah," *New Voices*, May 5, https://newvoices.org/2015/05/05/how-guilford-hillel-became-guilford-chavurah/

See also, a senior honors thesis written by Sara Minsky, the President of Hillel when the decision was made to join Open Hillel, "Narratives About Us, By Us: Progressive Jewish Groups in the United States Combatting Corporate Media," submitted in May 2015.

8 *Zionism: An Interlude*

AS THE DEBATE OVER Hillel and Open Hillel unfolded, it became apparent that some Jewish students were Zionists, some were anti-Zionists, and many (probably most) were not at all sure. I found myself thinking back to my childhood, when my parents never called themselves Zionists, but they assumed that Israel could do no wrong. Early political figures like Golda Meir, Abba Eban, and Moshe Dayan were revered, and when my parents put records on the record player, they were likely to include musicals like "Milk and Honey" (1961) and "Fiddler on the Roof" (1964). My parents were good liberals. They punished us, and chastised others, for using the Yiddish version of the n word ("schvartzes") when referring to African Americans (at that time, the term of choice was Negroes). Like most American Jews, they consistently voted for Democrats, including Adlai Stevenson rather than Eisenhower in 1952 and 1956 (they loved Stevenson—they would have been quite disappointed to learn, as I did later, that Stevenson, a graduate of Choate and Princeton, was prone to employ the same anti-Semitic language often used in the elite settings in which he was educated).[1] When I graduated from college in June 1967, and we packed up my parents' car with my worldly belongings to drive from Connecticut back to our home in Bethesda, MD, and we listened on the radio to news of the Israeli victory in the Six-Day War, they were jubilant.

I'm not sure when I became more critical of Israel, and more aware of the lives of Palestinians, but this probably happened gradually as Israel began to occupy more and more of the Palestinian territories, going against the wishes of the United Nations and, in many cases, the US government. As a regular subscriber to lefty magazines like *The Nation* and *Mother Jones*, but also the more moderate *New Yorker* and *New York Review of Books*, my views changed. While Lisa and I were in Middletown, Connecticut, in the fall of 1989, on one of the five sabbaticals I was privileged to have while teaching at Guilford, we heard a brilliant and riveting lecture by Edward Said, a Palestinian Professor of English and Comparative Literature at Columbia University (also a public intellectual of considerable renown). Although it was 31 years ago, I remember his talk quite vividly (including the room in which he spoke, where we were sitting, and the packed and intense audience), and I have no doubt that hearing Said's lecture, and his responses to questions, affected my thinking about Israel and Palestine. Reading books by Israelis, especially both the fiction and nonfiction of Amos Oz and Ari Shavit's *My Promised Land: The Triumph and Tragedy of Israel*,[2] also helped me realize the depth and complexity of the problems, and to understand more of the history that preceded the creation of the state of Israel in 1947. I had not started out as a Zionist, but, as I have indicated,

1. Baker, Jean H. 1997. *The Stevensons: A Biography*, New York: W. W. Norton, p. 252.
2. Shavit, Ari. 2013. *My Promised Land: The Triumph and Tragedy of Israel*, New York: Spiegel and Grau.

I grew up in a family that was devoted to Israel. I certainly was not an anti-Zionist.

In January 2020, browsing the new books in Greensboro's excellent public library, I saw a Yale University Press book by Susie Linfield titled *The Lions' Den: Zionism and the Left from Hannah Arendt to Noam Chomsky*.[3] I took it home and was fascinated by it. In the introduction, Linfield, a professor in the journalism department at NYU, describes eating dinner one night in 2012 with a group of left-wing academic friends. When one of them referred, disparagingly, to someone as a Zionist, and everyone but Linfield seemed to assume that this was definitely a disparaging accusation, she struggled with whether or not to speak up. She did: "Well so am I. I believe in a state for the Jewish people, along with a Palestinian one." This led to the project that resulted in her 2019 book. In it she details, and critiques, the views, sometimes the changing views, of many eminent left-wing intellectuals, including, as her subtitle indicates, Hannah Arendt and Noam Chomsky. This thorough and well-documented book did not convince me that I should be a Zionist, but it did persuade me that many leftist icons had changed their views over time, and that the issues were complicated.

In order to help me figure out how my childhood belief in the early dreams of Israel (as exemplified by the kibbutzim, Israel's socialist agrarian collectives) were in synch, or now out of synch, with the changing political realities, I turned

3. Linfield, Susie. 2019. *The Lions' Den: Zionism and the Left from Hannah Arendt to Noam Chomsky.* New Haven: Yale University Press, p. 1. Her critique of Chomsky is searing. For those who want to dig into the weeds of their disagreement, see Chomsky, Noam, "The truth about lies," *The Nation*, May 4/11, 2020, p. 2, Linfield, Susie, "The Source of our Disagreements," *The Nation*, June 1/8, pp. 2 and 26, and Chomsky, Noam, "Chomsky Responds," *The Nation*, June 1/8, 2020, p. 26.

to Jonathan Malino. Way back in 1982, when *Jews in the Protestant Establishment* was published, I gave a talk on campus in Founders Hall in what was called The Gallery (it is now Founders East Gallery). Jonathan introduced me. In thanking him for the nice introduction, I jokingly called him my "spiritual leader," an allusion to a Woody Allen routine in which Allen refers to his rabbi as his "spiritual leader" (in the routine, the punch line is Allen's discovery that, after having discouraged him from doing so, his rabbi appears in a vodka ad—Jonathan would never do that). I emailed Jonathan (now living in Canada), told him about Susie Linfield's book, and asked him if he considered himself a Zionist. His answer, classically Jonathan, was deeply thoughtful and nuanced. Here is what he wrote:

My ties to Israel are deeply rooted in childhood. The five happiest and freest months of my life were ones I spent in Jerusalem in 1956.

Ideologically, I suppose I've always been a Zionist, though I've never made much of the designation, since its meaning depends so heavily on contextual contrasts. I grew up in a household where support of Israel was constantly conjoined with criticism of Israeli policies and actions. My father, whose views on Israel became pretty much my own, had supported a bi-national rather than a Jewish State (the Brit Shalom movement), and I recall his preaching sermons in the early Fifties on the need for Israel to repatriate the refugees. So while we took great pride in Israel's accomplishments, the pride was always tempered by holding Israel to high moral standards. That said there was a deep naivete, evident in hindsight, in the hope/expectation that Israel would somehow succeed in being a more just country than others.

Today, the valence of "Zionism" has changed dramatically as Linfield's story makes clear. I wouldn't reject the label (and would argue that liberal or progressive Zionism need not be oxymoronic, however hard it is to imagine how it can be politically realized in today's world), but I would be quick to distance myself from the majority of those who embrace it. Their and my visions for Israel are radically disparate. And while the (critical) Zionism of my younger self came with pride and optimism, today it's conjoined with anguish and pessimism.

Finally, while I reject any conflation of anti-Zionism with antisemitism, I have no doubt that anti-Zionism is sometimes (often?) a cover for antisemitism, especially on the Left. (There's also the strange phenomenon of antisemitic Zionism on the Right, including, one might argue, among many Evangelicals.)

Unlike Jonathan, I did not spend blissful months in Jerusalem in 1956. By the summer of 1956 I was in my fifth year as a camper at Camp Airy, a Jewish camp in Thurmont, MD, that I went to from the age of seven until I was in my twenties, first as a camper and then as a counselor. Although it was a Jewish camp, and we had brief services each Friday night and Saturday morning, I don't recall much if any attention paid to Israel or to Zionism. So, although I didn't, like Jonathan, start out with a rabbi father, nor did I have a seminal childhood experience in Jerusalem, and I certainly can't say that "ideologically I suppose I have always been a Zionist," I can't improve upon his honest struggle with his Zionism and the "anguish and pessimism" that now accompanies it.

9 *Diya, Salaita, Bruce, and Jane*

IN BETWEEN THE DECISION in April 2014 by the Jewish students in Hillel to join Open Hillel, and the decision in March 2015 to call itself Chavurah, a lot happened on campus. One of the most anticipated, and controversial events was a visit by Steven Salaita on February 3rd.

Like Mohammed Abu-Nimer, the Palestinian faculty member who was at the college in the 1990s, Diya Abdo, a much-loved and gifted teacher, saw it as part of her educational mission to bring programs and speakers to the campus to provide perspectives that students and faculty might otherwise not encounter in traditional classes or the mainstream media. In the fall of 2014, she invited Steven Salaita, a Middle East scholar who had become a controversial and celebrated figure. Born in West Virginia to a Palestinian mother who was raised in Nicaragua and a Jordanian father, Salaita's extensive scholarship on themes of immigration, dislocation, indigenous peoples, race, and ethnicity led to a tenured position as an Associate Professor at Virginia Tech. A few years later, after a lengthy search, he was chosen from many applicants to join the American Indian

Studies Program at the University of Illinois, as a tenured professor. However, before he was able to do so, the University withdrew the offer because of a campaign against his hiring that was raised by pro-Israel students, faculty, and donors based on tweets that Salaita had made while at Virginia Tech which they saw as anti-Semitic.[1] Salaita's case generated considerable national attention, the University of Illinois was censured by the American Association of University Professors (AAUP), and the University of Illinois agreed to a $875,000 settlement (Salaita received $600,000 and his attorneys received $275,000).[2]

Salaita's talk was sponsored by the English Department, the Peace & Conflict Studies program, Friends Center, the Women's, Gender & Sexuality Studies Program and Students for Justice in Palestine (interestingly, one of the co-leaders of the Students for Justice in Palestine group was a Jewish student). There

1. Among Salaita's tweets were the following: "If you're defending #Israel right now you're an awful human being;" "This is not a conflict between #Israel and 'Hamas.' It's a struggle by an Indigenous people against a colonial power;" "If it's 'antisemitic' to deplore colonization, land theft, and child murder, then what choice does any person of conscience have?;" "Zionists: transforming 'antisemitism' from something horrible into something honorable since 1948;" "At this point, if Netanyahu appeared on TV with a necklace made from the teeth of Palestinian children, would anybody be surprised?" and "I refuse to conceptualize #Israel/#Palestine as Jewish-Arab acrimony. I am in solidarity with many Jews and in disagreement with many Arabs." Mackey, Robert. 2014. "Professor's Angry Tweets on Gaza Cost Him a Job," *New York Times*, September 12. https://www.nytimes.com/2014/09/13/world/middleeast/professors-angry-tweets-on-gaza-cost-him-a-job.html?_r=0
2. Cohen, Jodi S. 2015. "University of Illinois OKs $875,000 to end Steven Salaita Dispute," *Chicago Tribune*. November 12. https://www.chicagotribune.com/news/breaking/ct-steven-salaita-settlement-met-20151112-story.html

were some on campus who were opposed to Salaita's speaking, including at least one student,[3] and there were people in the local Jewish community who were opposed, including at least one major local donor to the college.

Salaita spoke to a packed house, a standing room only crowd in the Carnegie Room in the library. The talk was originally scheduled to take place in the Frank Family Science Center, a building that had been funded by the Frank family a few years after Stanley Frank died, but when one of the members of the family called Jane Fernandes, who had become the President of the college six months earlier, to complain about the talk being held in that building, she shifted the venue to the Carnegie Room.[4]

3. Weil, Josh. 2015. "Steven Salaita's visit promotes division in Guilford's community," *The Guilfordian*, Feb. 6. https://www. guilfordian.com/opinion/2015/02/06/letter-to-the-editor-steven-salaitas-visit-promotes-division-in-guilfords-community/

4. According to a local weekly magazine, *Yes Weekly*, Fred Guttman, the rabbi at Temple Emanuel, posted a message on Facebook in which he compared Salaita to a neo-Nazi member or a member of the Ku Klux Klan. See Abunimah, Ali. 2015. "North Carolina college bows to donor over Steven Salaita talk," *The Electronic Intifada*, February 2; https:// electronicintifada.net/blogs/ali-abunimah/north-carolina-college-bows-donor-pressure-over-steven-salaita-talk; see also, Abdo, Diya. 2015. "The most valuable lesson from Steven Salaita's visit to Guilford College," *The Electronic Intifada*, February 5; https://electronicintifada.net/content/most-valuable-lesson-steven-salaitas-visit-guilford-college/14246; and, see also, Jaschik, Scott. 2015. "Guilford moves lecture by Steven Salaita," *Inside Higher Education*, February 3, https://www.insidehighered.com/quicktakes/2015/02/03/guilford-moves-lecture-steven-salaita

By 2019, Salaita was no longer in academe—he was driving a school bus in the Washington D.C. area. Pettit, Emma. 2019. "'Ousted' from Academe, Steven Salaita Says He's Driving a School Bus to Make Ends Meet," *Chronicle of Higher Education*. February 19. https://www. chronicle.com/article/Ousted-From-Academe/245732

By this time, Bruce Stewart had retired from Sidwell Friends and was living in Chattanooga, Tennessee. On February 5, two days after Salaita's talk, Bruce forwarded to me an email that he had sent to Jane Fernandes. Bruce's email to Jane was titled "Concerns Regarding Atmosphere for Jewish Students at Guilford." In addition to his email, he also forwarded to Jane, and included in his email to me, an email that his wife had received from a former colleague, the mother of a then-current student at Guilford. The email from the mother had been sent to Jane, so when Jane got the email from Bruce she was receiving it for a second time. In his note to me, Bruce asked what I thought ("Richie, Any thoughts you have would be welcomed. This issue is of concern to me, but I am at some distance and have few details.").

First, let me summarize the letter that Bruce attached. The mother of the Guilford student had written previously to Jane, back in August, which means that her first email might have been one of the first ones Jane received when she began work at Guilford. In this second missive, the unhappy mother started by reminding Jane that she had written her in August, that Jane had written back, but, as she told Jane, "I'm afraid that my initial effort to communicate with you in August about my concern about the treatment and respect of Jewish students at Guilford wasn't given serious attention." She went on to express concern about "anti-Semitism on campus" and "the damage wrought by Max Carter." She clearly was not happy with Guilford, with Max, or with Jane: "I asked you in August for an action plan about changing this environment. You didn't produce that."

She also asked why Steven Salaita had been allowed to speak at Guilford: "If your administration is seriously interested in making this campus safe and accommodating for all students PEASE TELL ME WHY Steve Saliata [sic] was invited (and no doubt paid) to speak at Guilford? Please tell me why under your leadership you allowed this to take place?" Just to make sure that Jane knew she was serious, she concluded "I expect that you will respond with an action plan for changing this damaging campus environment. I am copying the president of the board of trustees because of the very serious nature of this issue."

Then there was Bruce's one-paragraph email to Jane, addressed "Dear President Fernandes" (notable because here in Quakerland we traditionally use first names—even the email from the angry mother began "Dear Jane"). Bruce then expressed his concern in no uncertain terms, and with a dose of what the Quakers call "eldering"—providing guidance in a firm, Quakerly, tone. He wrote: "I am VERY sorry that the environment of the College has grown to be so uncomfortable for so many Jewish students and for the broader Greensboro Jewish community. I have also heard from a local Greensboro Rabbi about his discomfort with the tone at the College regarding Middle Eastern issues, and from a Greensboro area attorney who is a personal friend. Since this matter of discourse is so highly sensitive to so many people, it seems very important to address it carefully, thoroughly and promptly. I hope Guilford College will do ALL that it can—and immediately—to resolve this issue in a fair, balanced and equitable manner."

So Jane got her second email from the angry mother, who assured her that she was copying email number two to the "president of the board of trustees" (there is no such position— she meant the chair of the board), Jane also got a terse eldering email from Bruce who assured her that he had spoken with a lawyer and a rabbi in Greensboro, and encouraged her to do ALL she could "and immediately" to address these issues.

Bruce asked me what I thought. Here is what I wrote him, later that same day:

Hi Bruce....

As to the many issues that you raise in your email to me and the one to Jane Fernandes, and other issues related to those you raise, I have many reactions. My take is quite different than that of xxxx (who I know—he was in one of my classes last semester) and his mother (who I don't know).

First, I think Max Carter has been unfairly vilified in the Greensboro Jewish community. I have the greatest respect for Max. He is a strong advocate for the rights of Palestinians, but, in my view, he has worked hard to allow for varied views about Middle East issues to be presented on campus. Max has traveled many times to Israel and to Palestine (most recently with Jonathan Malino this past January). I think Max is one of the most thoughtful, fair, and peaceful people I know, and I have been very disappointed by the tendency of some in the local Jewish community to demonize him (in her email, xxxx's mother refers to "the damage wrought by Max Carter").

As for Stephen Salaita, I have mixed feelings about the fact that he was denied an agreed-upon tenured position at the University of Illinois because of complaints about things he had tweeted (some of which were clearly quite inappropriate), but I have no mixed feelings at all about his speaking at Guilford. There were a number of panels and speakers on Middle East topics this past fall, some of which I attended. The "totally one-sided presentation" that xxxx's mother refers to included as one panelist the North Carolina head of Hillel (there were more people on that panel who were critical of Israel than who were supportive). A very strong (and hostile) pro-Israeli speaker named Edwin Black gave two talks while on campus this past November (this was his second visit to the campus). He apparently is so bombastic in his pro-Israel stance that some in the local Jewish community were embarrassed that he was invited—I note that xxxx's mother made no mention of that controversial, very pro-Israel talk on campus this past fall. I did not attend either of his presentations, but I was told that he was publicly quite aggressive in his hostility toward Max.

I had a class and was unable to attend Salaita's talk the other night, but otherwise I would have gone. Apparently his academic work (the work that got him tenure at Virginia Tech, and then, almost, a tenured position at the University of Illinois), compares the experiences of Palestinians to those of Native Americans (thus his appointment to the University of Illinois was to be in a Native American Studies department). It was videotaped and I plan to watch it. Friends on the faculty who were able to attend, and who I respect, tell me he gave a very impressive talk.

The Jewish community was indeed upset that Salaita was invited, and members of the Frank family asked that his talk not be held in the building they funded. I thought that Jane handled this well—she agreed to move the talk elsewhere, but she made it clear that if another venue had not been available she would not have canceled the talk.

I'm very sorry the Jewish community has come to see Guilford not only as anti-Israel but as anti-Semitic (I fear that, for some people, those who are critical of Israel are seen as anti-Israel, and for some people they are seen as anti-Semitic). Jonathan Malino now has retired, and I'm sorry that he is not here for as a rabbi and the son of a rabbi, he gave us some needed Jewish credibility; however, from what I hear from my friends in the Jewish community, because of Jonathan's willingness to criticize

Israel, some in the Jewish community see him as bad as, or worse than, Max Carter.

I don't know xxxx's mother, one of your key sources, but I do know xxxx. I'm sorry he is feeling disenchanted and alienated from the college, but I will say that of all the students in my classes last semester, xxxx held the strongest opinions, listened the least to others, and didn't show many indications of being especially thoughtful.

So, those are some thoughts inspired by your email. It is not news to me that the Greensboro Jewish community sees Guilford very negatively these days. Based on what I hear from colleagues at other schools, and what I read, many campuses are dealing with these same conflicts. As I said above, I think both Max Carter and Jane Fernandes have behaved admirably. Jane, of course, is in her first year, and she faces a mountain of challenges. I'm sorry to see this one added to her very full plate, but, as I've just suggested, there probably are few college presidents who will avoid this topic.

Glad to continue this conversation at some point. All the best to you, and Andra, and Kathleen.....

RICHIE

As if to provide additional emphasis to my having noted to Bruce that Max Carter and Jonathan Malino recently had traveled together to Israel and Palestine, and to demonstrate to the local Jewish community their ability to collaborate (birthright Quaker and rabbi), they wrote an article that appeared in the local paper on February 8, five days after Salaita's visit, three days after my email exchange with Bruce. The article, titled "More than 2 stories in Israel, Palestine," depicted the three weeks they had spent leading a group of students in January. Their main point, as suggested by the title of their article, was that there was not a single Israeli narrative, and not a single Palestinian narrative, but multiple narratives within each community. They emphasized that they "spent equal time among Jewish Israelis and Palestinians." They made no mention of Stephen Salaita, but they did note that "we heard from a leading opponent of the Boycott, Divestment and Sanctions movement and from one of BDS' founders."[5] It seemed to me as I read the article, and it seems to me as I read it again now, that it very much supports what I claimed about Max in my email to Bruce Stewart: he goes out of his way to be fair, he is thoughtful, and it is quite unfortunate that he has been vilified in the Greensboro Jewish community.[6]

Things seemed to get less intense after that, though maybe I just was out of the loop. There were some protests on campus, but the one I remember most clearly took place after a sexual harassment incident that occurred late one night, was reported to security about an hour later, and the person who made the complaint did not think they were treated with respect—especially because the head of security, an African American

5. Carter, Max L. and Jonathan W. Malino. 2015. "More than 2 stories in Israel, Palestine," *Greensboro News & Record*, February 8. https://www.greensboro.com/more-than-2-stories-in-israel-palestine/article_181f584c-e716-588d-a773-c603def6d7a7.html

6. Some people in the local Jewish community have accused Max Carter of being anti-Semitic. Some lobbied members of the administration and the board to get him fired. He tells me that when some people in the Jewish community actually have met him, rather than just hearing about him, they have said such things to him as "I just have to tell you that you are not as bad as I was led to believe," and "I thought you'd have horns." In another interesting turn-around, a few years later, having graduated, the son of the mother who wrote the angry letters to Jane profoundly apologized to Max for that episode and for having tried to get him fired.

man in his 60s, did not get the pronoun right. This led to a protest a few hours later, in the middle of the night, in which a group of students marched through the dorms beating pots and pans, waking many students up. A few hundred students gathered outside Founders Hall the next day, with some calling for Jane Fernandes to fire the head of security immediately, and other students expressing their outrage about having been awakened in the middle of the night. I did not hear a word about Israel or Palestine.

So, by the current academic year, 2019-2020, Jonathan had retired, and was living in Canada, and Max had retired (though he was still in Greensboro, and still taking groups to Ramallah). As often seemed to be the case, there were an indeterminate number of Jewish students on campus, a small and not very active Chavurah group, and some Palestinian students.

Two things took place in the spring of 2020 before the coronavirus changed everything (more on that anon). The first reminded me that we now have a fair number of Palestinian alumni. The second reminded me of the email that Bruce sent Jane back in 2015.

10   *The Palestinian Alumni*
      Make a Complaint

IN THE FALL OF 2019, a faculty member in the Business department (definitely not Jewish—or if he is, I completely give up on my Jewdar apparatus) traveled to Israel—which I only became aware of because the college public relations machine pumped out an article about the trip ("Michael Dutch Attends Bridge-Building Mission to Israel"). I was somewhat surprised that he was interested in Israel but didn't think much of it until one day I got a call from Frank Boyd, the provost, asking me to come by his office for a talk. He knew I was thinking about retiring, or perhaps reducing my teaching load from the 2/3 load it had been at for a while, and I assumed that was what he wanted to talk about.

To my surprise, he informed me that a group of more than 30 Palestinian alumni had written an angry letter to Jane Fernandes about this faculty member's trip to Israel. They were not upset that he had gone to Israel, but they were upset that the trip had been sponsored by the Jewish National Fund—USA (a group I knew nothing about) and publicized in such laudatory terms by the Guilford College public relations office. The Palestinian alumni also expressed concern about another trip taken by campus Quaker minister Wess Daniels that was sponsored by a local group called Interfaith Clergy Greensboro.[1] In their letter which I subsequently was able to see (addressed "Dear President Jane"), they wrote that they believed that these two trips were paid for by groups with particular political agendas and, as such, they should not be promoted by the Guilford public relations office in praiseworthy language:

> Established in 1901, JNF has been used effectively by Israelis to geoengineer historical Palestine and assert Israeli dominance over the landscape: an archetype of settler colonialism. Both of these trips are ventures by Zionist groups that seek to whitewash Israel and normalize the systemic injustices it exerts on Palestinians. Such trips are not innocent; they have political implications that grant Israel a carte blanche for its human rights violations. It sends a message that US academia at large, including Quaker institutions, will continue to treat it as a normal state, and not one of occupation and apartheid. This is not only immoral; it also goes against Guilford's legacy and core values.

Frank had asked to meet with me because he wanted to assure me that the college would strongly protect the freedom of a faculty member to travel anywhere (I had not read the

1. In 1992, Joanne Bluethenthal and Gail LeBauer presented a proposal to the Jewish Federation of Greensboro and the North Carolina Christians and Jews (NCCJ) to co-sponsor an interfaith study mission to Israel. The proposal was accepted, and the first trip took place in 1994. Subsequent trips have taken place in 1997, 1999, 2005, 2009, 2012, 2016, and 2019. Wess Daniels was one of the participants on the 2019 trip.

letter when we met, but he did not address the issue of how the college was to provide publicity about trips sponsored by organizations with particular political agendas). He also wanted to be sure that as a Jewish faculty member I felt comfortable in an atmosphere in which Palestinian students and alumni were voicing criticisms of Israel and the college. I assured him that I had never felt uncomfortable as a Jewish person on the campus, except when, as rarely happened, someone started talking about Jesus Christ as if everyone in the room believed in his divinity. Frank also had similar conversations with three of my Jewish colleagues.

Jane wrote back to the Palestinians, and they wrote her again. In addition to trying to process the arguments on both sides of the missives going back and forth (and trying not to lapse into my role as a teacher who was in the middle of a semester, grading hundreds of student papers, and thinking to myself, "I'd reword that," or "that sentence could use parallel construction"), I had two strong reactions. One was surprise that there were 30 Palestinian alumni who were active enough and organized enough to write such a letter (well, two letters.... so far). The other was sympathy for Jane Fernandes, thinking back to the angry letter from the Jewish mother that she received in her first weeks in the job, and to watching her on the front steps of Founders Hall trying to deal with angry protesting students who were calling for her to immediately fire the chief of security in part because of his inability to get the pronoun right. The President's office, I found myself thinking, must get a lot of incoming.

Probably every college President gets a lot of incoming, but it seems to me it must be especially hard to be the President of a liberal arts college like Guilford, with its Quaker history. There are, of course, many constituencies to deal with, including the usual groups found at any college: the students, parents, faculty, staff, and alumni. Guilford, in its own particular way, has the three constituencies I have focused on in this sort of a memoir: Quakers, Jews, and Palestinians. The Quakers think you need consensus. They may love silence, but they can be steel-willed in their convictions, as seen by the many Quaker abolitionists and conscientious objectors over the years. Their commitment to those convictions has sustained them in the face of serious pressure and even hostility from their communities, even during "popular" wars like World War Two. The Jews are willing, even eager, to argue.[2] The Palestinians? I don't know, but as their long and emotional emails to Jane in 2020 indicated, they have decades of grievances that have engendered strong convictions.

2. Jews argue? Max Carter tells me the following story: "Did I ever tell you about the time Rabbi Fred came storming over to campus demanding to see Jonathan and me about our programs? We met in the Hut, and I had the Hillel staff person there with me. She and I sat by the fireplace as Fred and Jonathan went at each other hammer and tong! At some point in the middle of their red-faced, vein-bulging tete-a-tete, they paused, looked over at me and my shocked expression, and said, 'You Quakers aren't used to this, are you?!'"

11 *The Lightbulb*

IN THE SPRING OF 2019, I received the Charles C. Hendricks '40 Distinguished Service Award. I was pleased and I was glad that I had decided to give up playing basketball that day to attend the luncheon at which I was honored. The recipients of the many other awards (the Young Alumni Achievement Awards, the Alumni Excellence Awards, the Honorary Alumnus Award, and the Community Cares Award) were very impressive, and I concluded that I was in very good company among those being honored. I was warmly and thoughtfully introduced by Sarah Estow, my (Jewish!) colleague, at the time the chair of the psychology department, and then I spoke for the two minutes that had been allotted to me, sharing some memories of Charlie Hendricks, and also saying a bit about his next door neighbor, Ed Burrows (I did not mention that Lisa and I light a yahrzeit candle every year for Ed). I knew that Lisa was planning to attend the luncheon, but I was touched that a number of others came to see me win this award, including Mark Dixon, a former student of mine who is now in the art department, Cyril Harvey (birthright Quaker), the Academic Dean when I was hired, and his wife,

Judy (convinced), Rob Luisana, one of my geezer basketball buddies, and Marie Branson Knapp, '83 (birthright Quaker), one of my all-time favorite former students who surprised me by flying down from New Jersey for the event. Although I realized, or maybe I should say although I had the cynical suspicion, that this event was part of a long-range fund-raising plan, whereby people who had been generous to the college were honored in the hopes that they would be even more generous in the future, I totally enjoyed myself and did in fact feel honored.

A few months later I was asked to be on the committee to select the 2020 recipients of the various awards. I did not see how I could refuse, so I agreed to serve on the six-member committee. We read the materials for the 30 or so people who were nominated for the various awards, and we came to agreement about which nominees to recommend to the two senior administrators who would make the final decisions, Jane Fernandes, the President, and Ara Serjoie, the Vice President for Advancement. In addition to the same awards that had been given in 2019, the committee was informed that in 2020 the college was adding a new award, the Lifetime Achievement Award. This new award was to recognize "Individuals who 1) have a long-term, demonstrated commitment to Guilford College; 2) have attained the highest level of accomplishment in their career; and 3) have wielded positive impact through civic and community engagement."

When the chair of the committee sent me an email asking what I thought about the nomination of a former Guilford administrator, now retired, for this award, I told her that he'd be okay but that a different former administrator, Bruce Stewart, would be the ideal person to receive it. She was new to the college and didn't know who Bruce was, so I told her that Bruce had been a Guilford undergraduate, had served in many administrative capacities over a 17-year period, had stepped in to save many a struggling person from crises of all sorts, and had been on the board of trustees, serving as its chair through an especially difficult time. I told her that I couldn't imagine anyone who had provided a lifetime of commitment to the college that could begin to compare with Bruce's. She encouraged me to go to the website and submit a nomination for Bruce in writing, which I did.

When the committee completed its work, it submitted Bruce's name to Jane and Ara, along with one of the other two people who had been nominated for the Lifetime Achievement Award. The other two nominees were quite impressive (one a Guilford graduate in the class of 1949 who became a physician, with a long career in radiology and nuclear medicine, the other a Holocaust survivor who graduated from Guilford in 1952 and then went on to a distinguished academic career). A few weeks later, when the chair sent those of us on the committee the final list of award winners, I saw that Bruce had not been chosen—the other two were to be the inaugural recipients of the Lifetime Achievement Award.

I was stunned. When next I spoke with the chair of the committee, I asked if she knew why Jane and Ara had rejected the committee's recommendation. She did not know. My initial thought, following my suspicions about the award ceremony as part of a broader fund-raising plan, was that the recipients were perhaps more likely to be major donors to the college than Bruce (not only might they have larger estates, but they were both in their 90s, so perhaps they were thought to be closer to meeting their maker and thus passing on those estates to someone or some institution). My next thought was that since Ara and Jane were both relatively new to Guilford, maybe they hadn't read the materials as closely as they could have, and perhaps didn't quite know who Bruce was, or how much and for how long he had contributed to the college.

And then, while working on this manuscript, and reading lots of old emails to try to clarify things Jewological rattling around in my head, lying awake in the middle of the night, the lightbulb went on. It wasn't that Jane didn't know who Bruce was. She probably remembered quite well that 2015 email from Bruce, and the email he forwarded to her and to me from the angry Jewish mother. If so, it may have been a very deliberate choice to give the award to a Holocaust survivor rather than to Bruce.

12 *Guilford's History, Guilford's Future*

JUST AS ARTHUR BLUETHENTHAL, a Jewish kid from Wilmington, NC, found his way to George School in the late 1930s, where he befriended Grimsley Hobbs, twenty-five years later Ed Winslow, a Quaker kid from Tarboro, NC, found his way to Westtown, another Quaker boarding school near Philadelphia. Years later, a partner in a Greensboro law firm, Winslow became a member of, and then the chair of, the board of trustees at Guilford College.[1] In April 2020, a month or so into the shutdown of the college due to the coronavirus, the faculty held a meeting via Zoom in order to ask questions of Jane Fernandes about the budget crisis the college faced (even before the virus hit), and emerging plans for the uncertain future. Winslow was one of a handful of board members to Zoom into the meeting. After a moment of silence, and before the faculty's questions were

1. According to one of my (impeccable) sources, Edward C. Winslow III was a birthright Quaker. However, by the time he became chair of the board at Guilford he had become an Episcopalian. He then started attending New Garden Meeting. Therefore, by my calculations, he is both a birthright and a convinced Quaker.

addressed to Jane Fernandes, Jim Hood, the clerk of the faculty, asked Winslow to say a few words.

He began by praising the faculty for its dedicated work over the previous eight months in shifting to a dramatically new curriculum called the EDGE and a dramatically new schedule (a schedule, he did not mention, that most faculty had strongly opposed, and one that in its first year had been for the most part quite unpopular with both students and faculty). He praised the faculty for the diligent and creative work they had done to move their classes online in the middle of the semester because of the coronavirus, and he praised Jane Fernandes and her "Cabinet" for their excellent leadership before and during the current crisis. He then informed the faculty that he wanted to put to rest the rumors that college money had been embezzled (the board, he explained, had hired someone to look into this, and there was no evidence of anything inappropriate). Finally, Winslow turned to a historical perspective. He said that although two histories of the college had been written, they were now "long in the tooth," and "we need a new history" (my ears perked up). He went on to say that when it was written, he was sure that there would be a chapter on this coronavirus.

After my ears perked up, I found myself laughing out loud—luckily my microphone was muted. I laughed because for some time I had fantasized about writing an underground history of the college, one that would include the kind of stuff that those two previous "serious" histories had left out.[2] For example, it

2. Those two histories are Thorne, Dorothy Gilbert. 1937. *Guilford: A Quaker College*, Greensboro, NC: Guilford College; and Stoesen, Alexander R. 1987. *Guilford College: On the Strength of 150 Years*, Greensboro, NC: Guilford College. There is a third, more recent, history, not book-length, but a chapter in a book. See Erickson, Gwen, 2007. "Guilford College," in *Founded by Friends: The Quaker Heritage of Fifteen American Colleges and Universities*, edited by John W. Oliver, Jr., Charles L. Cherry, and Caroline L. Cherry (21-42). Lanham, MD: The Scarecrow Press.

would include the time two art students were arrested for posing nude by the side of Interstate 40, in broad daylight, for a photography session, or the time after 9-11 when a Guilford senior was arrested for smuggling a box cutter onto an airplane just to show that the security wasn't all that good, or the time the president of the student body, in the midst of a reelection campaign, faked being knocked unconscious and having "nigger lover" written on her chest with a red marker (she won the election).[3] These are just some of the student stories—the faculty ones are even better.

If Guilford survives, no sure thing, if it remains at all true to its heritage there will be Quaker faculty and students, and I hope there will be Jewish and Palestinian faculty and students.

In the spring of 2020, the Religious Studies department offered a course by Marilyn Forman Chandler, the long-time Executive Director of the Greensboro Jewish Federation, titled "Judaism: Food, Film and Festivals." It also offered a class by Hadia Mubarak, a woman born and raised in Florida to Jordanian and Syrian parents, titled "Women and Gender in Islam." The 2020 summer schedule included a course taught by Zulfiya Tursunova, a Russian-born professor of Peace and

3. No kidding—here are some references. Simmons, Kelly. 1993. "Two Students Charged with Indecent Exposure/Guilford College Students," *Greensboro News & Record*, Feb. 22, https://www.greensboro.com/two-charged-with-indecent-exposure-guilford-college-students/article_0575aa27-d9fe-5303-aacc-618c05aaff4f.html; Rich, Eric. 2004. "Student who hid box cutters on BWI flight gets probation, *Washington Post*, June 25, https://www.washingtonpost.com/archive/local/2004/06/25/student-who-hid-box-cutters-on-bwi-flight-gets-probation/e0e3337d-cea9-427b-b203-401d0bbf747f; and "Guilford College student who reported racial attack apologizes," *Chronicle of Higher Education*, July 3, 1998, https://www.chronicle.com/article/Guilford-College-Student-Who/99234

Conflict Studies, who earned her Ph.D. in Manitoba, Canada, titled "War and Peace in the Middle East."

Guilford has come a long way since its all-white days that only ended in the 1960s after Grimsley Hobbs became President. It has done for its students, and for the wider community, what any real college does—it has taught a wide range of challenging courses, including some on controversial topics, it has raised questions students have not thought to ask or have not wanted to ask, and it has encouraged them to challenge the status quo. Obviously some Quakers have been doing these things for a long time, though this does not seem to have characterized Guilford College in the 1950s. I am convinced that including Jews and Palestinians in the Guilford community, even though or perhaps because they don't agree with one another (or among themselves) has made the college a much more vibrant place, a much better liberal arts school than it would have been without them.

Epilogue

The 2020–21 Academic Year: AAUP and "Save Guilford College"

WITH DECLINING ENROLLMENTS, Guilford College was in financial trouble before the coronavirus. It was not the only school dealing with the double whammy of previous financial woes and COVID-19, and it was not the only school that took this double whammy as an opportunity to use questionable tactics when it came to shared governance and tenure protections. In late May, 2021, the American Association of University Professors (AAUP) published a report based on the widespread attacks on faculty governance and tenure protections that took place during the pandemic. It highlighted eight schools that, as the report put it, had used the pandemic as an "opportunity to turbocharge the corporate model." It went on to assert that these schools had laid off faculty members "as expeditiously as if colleges and universities were businesses whose CEOs suddenly decided to stop making widgets or shut down the steelworks." [1]

1. Flaherty, Colleen. 2021. "'A Watershed Moment' for Shared Governance," *Inside Higher Ed*, May 26, 2021. https://www.insidehighered.com/news/2021/05/26/aaup-finds-major-erosion-shared-governance-during-covid-19

Fortunately Guilford was not one of them.

I am convinced Guilford barely escaped this AAUP list of dishonor because of the extensive and creative efforts on the part of the newly energized AAUP chapter. One of the many actions taken by the AAUP was a virtual teach-in on October 21, 2020, that inspired the formation of a group called "Save Guilford College" (SGC). SGC ultimately included thousands of alumni and friends of the school. Guilford has not (yet) gone over the cliff, but, to mix my geographical metaphors, it is not out of the woods. In my view, the AAUP and SGC deserve a great deal of credit.

Before the deluge

For a number of years prior to the pandemic, details about the budget had not been shared, and neither the president nor the board of trustees had revealed just how precarious things were. When the virus hit, what was already a dire situation became a crisis, and the scope of the economic challenges became more apparent. It was known that the board had borrowed a good deal of money. Faculty and staff were shocked and dismayed to learn just how much debt had been taken on without, as in the past, broad community discussion. Between 2016 and 2018, the college, with an endowment at the time of about $70 million, borrowed $73 million. As the school faced up to preparing its 2021-22 budget, it became clear that a big chunk, over $5 million (more than 10% of the annual budget) was needed to pay the debt service on the money borrowed. Faculty and staff were even more upset when they learned that because the school had mostly tapped out its capacity to borrow more, in order to secure some of these loans the board had been willing to use the school's 335 acres of woods as collateral.

I found this especially painful. Long ago, in November 1973, when I came to Greensboro from Santa Cruz, CA, to interview for a position in the psychology department, I wanted to know how solvent the school was. I asked Cyril Harvey, then the Academic Dean, the size of the school's endowment. Somewhat sheepishly he acknowledged that it was very small, only about $5 million, but he assured me that Guilford College was quite stable financially. He went on to point out that Quakers are very cautious about borrowing money, and that Guilford thus far had avoided debt. Moreover, he said, the school sits on very valuable real estate, including hundreds of acres which make up the college woods (these woods had been an important stop on the Underground Railroad). The size of the debt the school had taken on between 2016 and 2018, coupled with the use of the college woods to secure the loans, brought back vivid memories of that 1973 conversation.

Although some of the borrowed money was used for what the board designated as "essential renovations," some was used for new construction that may or may not have been "essential," including a new ceramics building near the existing art building, and what is called "The Orangerie," an 1,100 square-foot glassed-in outdoor supplemental "study and social space" adjacent to an existing dorm. Some money was used to finance the considerable costs related to the newly adopted calendar and curriculum.

Therefore, even before March 2020, given the decline in enrollment and the level of debt, the school was in deep financial trouble. Many were worried that the college's administration and board were not up to the task of bringing it through the additional challenges of the coronavirus.

For the previous few years, Guilford College had a nominal chapter of AAUP, with a handful of dues-paying members, and a handful of other faculty supporters who had decided not to pay, or not gotten around to paying, their annual dues. In 2008, I had helped resuscitate the chapter (there had been a chapter in the 1980s), and for about a dozen years I was the chapter president (I was tenured, and relatively secure; many of the other AAUP members were not tenured, and some were anxious about taking on a highly visible leadership role). Some years we were more active than others. Often we chose to focus on a single issue, such as the college's treatment of contingent faculty, or gender differences in compensation.

Even when there were relatively few members, we kept the chapter going, in part because I naively believed that the very existence of an AAUP chapter on campus functioned as a deterrent. No school, especially a somewhat progressive one like Guilford, with its admirable Quaker values, wanted to be on the AAUP list of censured administrations. I therefore thought, and sometimes said, that the college's senior administrators would not do anything especially egregious. I was proven to be wrong about this a number of times, such as when the administration, during the summer vacation in 2009, without the approval of the faculty, agreed to a $500,000 grant from the BB&T Foundation that required teachers in certain classes to assign Ayn Rand's *Atlas Shrugged*, a lengthy, polemical novel that endorses individualism, justifies selfishness, and idealizes capitalism (according to the agreement, students were required to read this very long novel "in its entirety").[2]

In October 2018, I had tried to reactivate our dormant chapter, but few of my colleagues were interested in doing so. The following year, in December 2019, as financial matters and questions about the college's leadership had become more worrisome, I tried again. This time I had the support of an adjunct faculty member who had been quite active at the AAUP chapter where he previously taught, and who turned out to have valuable organizing skills. I invited the seven or eight card-carrying AAUP members and some others who had supported

2. Zweigenhaft, Richie. 2010. "Is This Curriculum for Sale?" *Academe*, 96 (4), 38–39. July–August, 2010. https://www.aaup.org/article/curriculum-sale

our chapter in the past to a meeting in early January 2020 at Scuppernong, Greensboro's local independent bookstore. This time there was sufficient interest, and some of those who attended were willing to assume leadership roles (I was soon to turn 75, and thinking about retiring). The wheels were set in motion. It was a good thing, for the shit was soon to hit the fan, and little did I realize that a newly formed AAUP chapter would play such a crucial role in saving the college.

March 2020: Covid

In mid-March, 2020, during the school's spring break, Jane Fernandes, who had been president since 2014, announced that the spring break would be extended for an additional week, and that all courses would then be shifted to an online format for the following two weeks. It was pretty clear that this change to online teaching was likely to last for much longer than two weeks, and indeed it did—it lasted the rest of the semester, and most of the 2020-2021 academic year. I was teaching two classes, both of which were going well.

I hated that I could no longer meet in the same room with my students, though they were diligent and did their best to complete the semester online. Still, it was not the same—neither as fun nor as gratifying as teaching face-to-face. Retirement became more appealing because I did not want to conclude my teaching career online. Moreover, and more importantly, I suspected that because of the existing financial crisis at the college, compounded by whatever financial pressures the coronavirus was going to bring, Guilford would soon furlough and perhaps terminate the contracts of faculty and staff. I did not want to be drawing my endowed professor salary when my younger, less well-paid, colleagues lost their jobs. I decided to retire.

That spring and early summer was filled with uncertainty throughout the country (indeed, throughout the world), and things were especially chaotic at the college. As I have noted, we were in the midst of the first year of a new calendar (a block calendar, with two three-week intensive sessions, during which students took only one class that met each day for three hours, and two twelve-week sessions, during which students took three classes). It had been imposed by the president against the wishes of the faculty. She had been persuaded by a report written by an outside consultant group that in recent years had encouraged a number of other colleges to adopt similar block calendars (with mixed results). Guilford was also in the first year of a radical new curriculum, one that the faculty had been pressured to adopt, and which it had done only reluctantly. Some students were on the old curriculum, and some were on the new one. Both the calendar and the curriculum had caused considerable confusion among students and faculty alike. Moreover, whether classes in the fall of 2020 would have to take place online, when students would be allowed to return to the campus, and what kinds of hybrid options might be possible, remained unclear.

Furloughs and terminations, round one

On April 2, 2020, Fernandes announced that the next day 133 full-time and part-time staff members (about one third of the college's work force) would be placed on furlough for two months; these furloughs were subsequently extended to July 31. There was no published list of who was furloughed. Sometimes the only way to learn that someone had been furloughed was when an email was returned. For example, I received this from the campus minister: "Thank you for contacting me. I am currently on furlough and am unavailable."

As a Quaker-affiliated school, Guilford does not have a faculty senate with a president elected by the faculty. Instead it has a clerk elected by the faculty (one of the rare occasions when the faculty votes, as most decisions are made by consensus), a clerk's committee, and monthly meetings of the corporate faculty. On May 17, Frank Boyd, the provost and Vice President for Academic Affairs, who was in his third year at Guilford, sent an email to the community in which he announced his resignation. He did not give a reason for his sudden resignation, but I assumed that he was unhappy with the direction the college was going, and that as the chief academic officer he did not feel that he was being heard when he tried to represent the viewpoints and interests of the faculty and preserve the integrity of the academic program.

In part because of this resignation, but also encouraged by members of the now-active AAUP chapter over what was assumed to be widespread faculty unhappiness with the college's leadership, the clerk's committee decided to survey all tenured, tenure-track, non-tenure-track full-time, and part-time faculty teaching that semester. The results demonstrated quite clearly that very few on the faculty had confidence in the president. In response to a question that asked "If the faculty were to take a vote of no confidence in President Jane Fernandes this week...," 55% reported that they would "definitely" vote no-confidence, and another 22% reported that they would "probably" vote no confidence. In late May, a report based on the survey was sent to the president, members of the board of trustees, and the faculty. It concluded that "most faculty lack confidence in President Fernandes' competency, leadership skills, financial literacy and are frustrated with the lack of transparent communication, ethical leadership, and commitment to shared governance."

With clear evidence that she had so little faculty support, and presumably less and less support from the board, on June 26 Fernandes announced her decision to step down (the board may have pressured her to do so). She would continue as president until July 31, spend a year on sabbatical, and return to the college as a tenured member of the English department in the fall of 2021.[3]

Round two, more terminations

On July 1 (Fernandes was still in office, and a search was ongoing for an interim replacement for her), 45 staff were let go, as were 5 visiting faculty. As students and alumni learned that programs they valued had been eliminated or cut drastically, or that favorite faculty or staff were gone, they expressed their unhappiness in a variety of ways.

Adding insult to injury, the process by which faculty and staff were furloughed or terminated was ham-handed, to say

3. Fernandes did not return to teach at Guilford. On August 4, 2021, Antioch College in Ohio, which closed in 2008 and reopened in 2011 under new management, announced that Jane Fernandes had been appointed as the school's third president since its relaunch in 2011. In the 2020–21 academic year, Antioch had 21 faculty and fewer than 100 students. Antioch College is separate from Antioch University (in 2009, Antioch University granted the college the rights to use the name Antioch College). Charlotte Roberts, a member of the Guilford Board of Trustees from 1997 to 2009, and in 2010 became a member of the Antioch University Board of Governors (she was the chair of that board in 2017). Martha Summerville, a member of the Guilford Board of Trustees from 1999 to 2008, and from 2009 to 2018, has been on the Antioch University Board of Governors since 2014.

By mid-August, 2021, four of the vice presidents in Fernandes' Cabinet had announced that they were leaving Guilford: Frank Boyd, the Vice President for Academic Affairs and Provost, resigned his position in May 2020 and then took an early retirement option; Ara Serjoie, Vice President for Advancement, took a position at Haverford College; Barbara Lawrence, Vice President of Diversity, Equity, and Inclusion, accepted a position at Ryder University in New Jersey, and Roger Degerman, Vice President of Marketing and Enrollment, took a similar position at Simpson College in Indianola, Iowa.

the least. Some employees learned of their furloughed status through reports in the media, others via emails, many were not sure if they had or had not been furloughed, and those who were furloughed did not know if or when they would be able to return to work. Some of those who lost their jobs were given a few minutes to collect their things, were escorted off campus, and were told they could not come back on campus without permission. That is, they were treated as if they were, or might become, criminals. Perhaps following the advice of the college's lawyer, or maybe just following the trend of colleges to treat employees as they often are treated in the corporate world, the school had adopted this practice some years earlier. In addition to being told they could not come on campus without permission, many employees were required to sign non-disclosure clauses in order to receive severance pay.

Many in the larger Guilford community were especially upset because such treatment violated the college's oft-professed commitment to Quaker values. In one letter to the board, a group of professors emeriti emphasized that non-disclosure and non-disparagement agreements make "a travesty of Quaker values:"

> We find it wholly unacceptable that in order to receive severance pay, some former employees must sign, by an August deadline, a contract with a non-disparagement clause. For the employee to say to anyone beyond the circle of family and friends that "I just signed an agreement that I believe to be counter to the college's stated value of integrity" would violate that clause. Moreover, the contract requires the signer to refrain from speaking about any matters related to their sphere of work with anyone except current college employees "with a need to know." A former employee with knowledge needed by the board could not, without violating the agreement,

speak even to a trustee about matters of mutual concern. Believing that integrity requires speaking when led to do so, without malicious intent and truthfully, how can a person sign in good faith such a travesty of Quaker values? We urge the board to rescind these conscience-insulting requirements.

The clerk's committee also called for an end to such practices. In a June 6 memo sent to the board, that committee called for the school to "Release parties at Guilford bound by non-disclosure agreements related to potential claims against the College."

On July 6, I, too, wrote Ed Winslow, the chair of the board, expressing my dismay at such treatment. Knowing that the board had announced that it planned to appoint an interim president to replace Fernandes while gearing up for a national search for a new president, I emphasized to Winslow that it was crucial to choose someone who knew the school well and who already had the trust of the Guilford community. More specifically, I recommended Jim Hood, a long-time member of the English department, a recent clerk of the faculty, a Guilford alumnus, and a birthright Quaker. Though I am not a Quaker (nor have I ever pretended to be), I stressed that recent abhorrent behavior by the administration and questionable decisions by the board had very much underscored the importance of the school regaining its Quaker values, values that are often promoted in public relations communications, but in the minds of many had been woefully lacking in the school's actions. My email to Winslow included the following:

Jim, more than anyone else on campus (including other faculty, and definitely including the current administrators in Jane's cabinet), has the widespread respect and support of the faculty. Moreover, I think it would be a plus that he is a Quaker. I was not against hiring a non-Quaker president in each of our last two presidential searches, but I think the concerns that I have expressed above about the way we have come to treat employees (not only, but especially, when they are fired), reflects the loss over time of some important Quaker values. As you presumably know, we have very few Quakers on campus these days (fewer than 10 now, down from 30–40 in the 1980s and 1990s, and only three Quakers on the full-time faculty).

The board was getting inundated by emails, from individuals and groups, about a range of issues, not just the shoddy treatment of furloughed and fired employees and recommendations about who might make a good interim president. One open letter to the board, signed by 900 alumni, encouraged the college to save money by cutting the pay of all administrators who made more than $100,000 ("Executives making six-figure salaries should not 'reduce' employees barely making a living wage without first slashing their own salaries to $100,000, at most"). Another group of 30 Quakers (weighty Quakers, as they say), that included former employees, alumni, three former members of the board of trustees, and two former presidents of the college (Bill Rogers, who was president 1980 to 1996, and Don McNemar, president from 1996-2002), sent a letter that urged the board to reverse a recent decision that changed the supervision of the Friends Center, responsible for Quaker teaching and programming on and off campus, from the college president to another campus office and one of the vice-presidents (they feared that this change reflected, and might add to, the decline in Quaker values at the school). The board also received emails from the executive committee of the Friends Association for Higher Education, the General

Secretary of the American Friends Service Committee, the Association of American Historians, and from AAUP members and entire AAUP chapters throughout the state. Some of those who wrote to the board submitted their letters as letters to the editor or as guest columns in the local newspaper. The board was getting lots of mail, and Guilford was not getting good press.

In its search for a president, the board used The Registry, an organization founded in 1992 and now a subsidiary of Collegiate Enterprise Solutions, LLC, described by *Inside Higher Education* as "an interim professional matchmaking organization that helps college boards fill presidential and administrative vacancies." On July 27, Winslow announced that the school had hired Carol Moore, a former high school teacher and biology professor who had served as president of three colleges over the previous decades, including Burlington College in Vermont (which subsequently closed) and Columbia College in South Carolina (still going, and from which she had retired three months earlier due to "family and health reasons"). Although I was not the only person to have nominated Jim Hood, he was not one of the three finalists interviewed for the job, and in fact he did not receive either a phone call or an email from the board's search committee about the position (but, stay tuned, because seven months later, in February 2021, after the board apparently pressured Carol Moore to step down, Jim Hood was to become the interim president).

So, with the provost suddenly and unexpectedly having resigned, the president having announced that she was taking a year-long sabbatical, the board having hired a new unknown interim president whose specialty was trying to save schools from going under, and the board only recently having revealed just how much money the school had borrowed (and the size of the college's annual debt-service payment), it felt like Guilford was heading toward the cliff.

. Things soon got worse.

It did not take long to see that Carol Moore had an agenda. Because of the college's pressing debt, she had no doubt that in order to pay the bills it would have to cut programs and terminate the contracts of many faculty and staff. The question for her seemed to be, simply, which programs and which employees. She believed that in order to attract more students, Guilford would have to offer new programs that students and their families were willing to pay for, but she acknowledged that it would take some time to develop and market such programs. In preparing for the immediate cuts that she saw as inevitable, she took some perfunctory steps to include faculty. On a very tight time-line, she asked each department to submit a report that detailed its contributions to the college. Although these reports were to include narrative assessments, it was apparent that the key data that would be of primary importance were the number of majors and average class sizes.

She then asked the curriculum committee and the clerk's committee to use those reports to prioritize—which programs and departments were to stay and which were to go? Both committees challenged her assumption that cutting was the only way to save money, even in the face of an immediate economic crisis, and instead the two committees developed and proposed a lengthy list of alternatives. In an email, the chair of the curriculum committee encouraged the faculty to contribute to an emerging list of "Creative Ideas that don't involve laying off faculty," with three categories: "Ideas that would reduce employee compensation," "Ideas that would reduce other expenses," and "Ideas that would generate more revenue." The final list that the committee submitted to Carol Moore included implementing an early retirement program, asking faculty if they were willing to take a voluntary year's leave, or if they were willing to teach and be paid at a two-thirds rate. It also included proposals capping all salaries, as well as proposals for progressive cuts to the salaries of the highest paid administrators. Despite what were in fact serious and in some cases creative proposals to come up with alternatives to a slash and burn approach, Moore's response was to belittle these efforts. As a writer for the *Wall Street Journal* put it, "Dr. Moore said she asked for faculty input, and 'they sent a nice note back saying don't cut anything.'" [4] (Again, stay tuned, for many months later, after Jim Hood succeeded Carol Moore as interim president, some of these very same proposals were put into practice.)

Round three, the ax falls

In early November Moore proposed to the board that the college eliminate 19 majors. These included many in the humanities and social sciences (history, political science, economics, philosophy, religious studies, creative writing, sociology/ anthropology, community and justice studies, peace and conflict studies, and modern languages), but it also included majors in math and the sciences (forensic biology, chemistry, geology, and physics). She also announced that another 27 faculty members, nearly a third of the faculty, would be fired, including 16 who were tenured. Among those who were to lose their jobs were some who held endowed professorships, some who had won teaching awards, and four long-term visiting professors who had been teaching full-time at the school for more than a decade. Eight of those fired had been at the college for more than 20 years, three for more than 30 years.

I suspect that the board hired Moore not only because of her alleged expertise saving colleges in trouble, but also because she

4. Belkin, Douglas. 2020. "Hit by Covid, Colleges do the Unthinkable and Cut Tenure," *Wall Street Journal*, December 6, 2020. https://www.wsj.com/articles/hit-by-covid-19-colleges-do-the-unthinkable-and-cut-tenure-11607250780

did not know any of the people that the school would need to furlough and fire. As these decisions were seen to be inevitable, the board may have assumed that in order to make such difficult decisions it was better to have someone in charge without close personal ties than someone who knew those who were losing their jobs. Moore had been at the school less than four months and, although she lived some of the time in an on-campus house for the college president (Ragsdale House), because of the pandemic she spent a fair amount of time in South Carolina. When she was in Greensboro, the campus was mostly empty, as students and faculty were no longer there. In all likelihood, she had never been in the same room as any of those who received termination letters. She was not part of the community, and the "objective" and distant tone that she adopted in written communications about the decisions she made reflected that.

Even though these cuts had not yet been formally approved by the board, Moore sent termination letters and posted a statement about these terminations on the college website. Her posted statement included the following: "Change can cause anxious moments, but it is also a time of opportunity. Over the next weeks and months, we will be turning our attention to developing the College's future path. Indeed, the Futures Task Force has already begun that work, and we look forward to sharing information with you as it develops. While much of this change is exciting, the discontinuation of some majors will result in the loss of some of the College's faculty members at the end of this academic year."

That final phrase, "at the end of this academic year," was yet another source of anger toward Moore and toward the college. Only a few weeks earlier, at a virtual community meeting, in speculating on the increasingly likely possibility that tenured faculty would lose their jobs, Moore was asked if they would have only to the end of the spring semester or if they would have two more semesters, and thus still be employed by the college in the fall of 2021. She replied that when circumstances dictated that it was necessary to fire tenured faculty, the convention in academia is to give a year's notice. However, a few weeks later in another virtual meeting, when she was asked about the fact that those who had received termination letters were given only one, not two semesters, she said that she (and presumably the college lawyer) had found that the wording in the Guilford College Handbook was ambiguous on this matter, and therefore in order to save more money the decision had been made to give the fired tenured faculty only one semester, not two. Needless to say, in a very difficult job market, with schools all over the nation cutting back rather than expanding, this made it even less likely that the fired tenured faculty would be able to find academic jobs elsewhere.

According to the school's handbook, and according to AAUP guidelines, tenured faculty cannot be fired unless the school declares "financial exigency" (that is, an imminent financial crisis). The concern is that colleges will use what may be financial challenges, but not bona fide crises, to fire tenured faculty either as cost-saving efforts or to get rid of those who have in some way irritated those in power. Carol Moore and the board worried that a public declaration of financial exigency would create bad press that could hurt enrollment, and might lead to problems with the Southern Association of Colleges and Schools (SACS), the school's accrediting agency.

In the individual letters that she sent to the terminated faculty on November 6, Moore also included the esoteric phrase, "there are no bumping rights." Apparently she wanted to be sure they knew that they would not have the right, as stipulated in some labor contracts, to take the jobs of less senior employees (thus bumping the firing to those hired more recently). Mainly, though, in addition to confusing most of those who received the letters (they had no idea what "bumping rights" were), her decision to include this in her letter demonstrated quite clearly that she held a corporate, not an academic, mindset. She had been hired by the board to balance the budget and to her, and apparently to the board, that meant cutting programs and faculty. Indeed, at this point the chair of the board had only praise for Moore and her plan. He told a reporter for the local paper that he was impressed that Moore had taken "such decisive action so quickly," and he said, apparently speaking for the board, "We're very pleased with Carol's leadership."[5]

On November 11, 2020, less than a week after the termination letters were mailed, the faculty voted no confidence in Carol Moore. It is not so rare for college faculties to vote no confidence in their presidents, though this was the first time it had happened in Guilford's 183-year history.[6] Guilford's faculty, however, also took the more unusual step of voting no confidence in the "leadership of the board" (which rankled some board members a good bit). These votes were not even close: 94% voted no confidence in Carol Moore, and 93% voted no confidence in the leadership of the board.[7]

5. Newsome, John. 2020. "'Heartbreaking:' Guilford College to make deep cuts to its academic majors and faculty," News & Record, November 6, 2020. https://greensboro.com/news/local/education/heartbreaking-guilford-college-to-make-deep-cuts-to-its-academic-majors-and-faculty/article_7755e64e-1f88-11eb-8cf0-4743eb7847ae.html

6. In May 2020 the clerk's committee surveyed the faculty about the possibility of a vote of no confidence, but no vote was actually taken.

7. Newsome, John. 2020. "The Syllabus: A no-confidence vote in Guilford College's Leadership." News & Record. November 17, 2020. https://greensboro.com/blogs/the_syllabus/the-syllabus-a-no-confidence-vote-in-guilford-colleges-leadership/article_05888894-25e8-11eb-948c-e701522dfa6e.html; and Whitford, Emma. 2020. "Deep Budget and Program Cuts Roil Guilford," Inside Higher Ed, November 23, 2020. https://www.insidehighered.com/news/2020/11/23/rare-no-confidence-vote-highlights-division-over-cuts-guilford-college

AAUP, newly energized, up and running

The new chapter of the AAUP hit the ground running. At the planning meeting held at the local bookstore in January 2020, those gathered had selected four officers (a tenured professor of chemistry, a tenured professor of philosophy, a tenured professor of geology, and an adjunct full-time assistant professor of criminal justice). They then arranged for the newly written by-laws to be approved by the national office in Washington, D.C., and the members of the new chapter began to meet regularly, by Zoom. Soon there were 36 dues-paying members, far more than ever before (evidence of effective organizing, but also of the immediacy of the looming crisis). In addition to the officers meeting frequently, every week or two, the group held Zoom meetings open to all members. Typically, between 15 and 25 people Zoomed in to discuss rumors, to deconstruct things that actually had happened, and to plan for future actions. The group worked hard to publicize not only that many academic and non-academic programs were at great risk of being eliminated, and that many employees had been or soon would be furloughed or fired, but that the processes employed had violated AAUP guidelines, the college's own guidelines, and the school's professed Quaker values.

In addition to the predictable letters to the editor, press releases, and individual and group letters to Guilford's president (and, subsequently, to the interim president), and to the board, AAUP members came up with some creative efforts that generated considerable publicity both locally and nationally. For example, after the second round of terminations, in early July, the AAUP arranged for a symbolic protest on campus in which rows of empty chairs were placed outside one of the campus buildings, each chair bearing the job title of an employee who had been terminated. The photo was widely shared on social media, and when the *Chronicle of Higher Education* ran an article in November 2020, titled "Colleges Have Shed a Tenth of Their Employees Since the Pandemic Began," it used the photo to introduce the article.[8] In another creative move, the AAUP chapter put together a poster, one that looked like a "most wanted" poster, but it included the smiling faces of "Guilford Faculty Targeted for Termination." This, too, made its rounds on social media, and alerted many alumni and others in the college community just who had been targeted by this decision (see the the flyer in Appendix 3, and the photo in Appendix 4). In its use of the photo and the poster, and in other ways, Guilford's AAUP activists employed a savvy use of social media, one that spread the growing concerns about the direction the school was heading far and wide among students, faculty, staff, alumni, parents, and others who care about Guilford.

Guilford's AAUP chapter was inspired by some creative efforts that had been employed in recent years by AAUP chapters at other North Carolina schools. For example, in a protest over the decision by the administration not to raise faculty salaries (when they had raised administrative salaries), the Appalachian State University AAUP chapter used many creative strategies, including a campaign in which thousands of postcards were mailed to the provost, generating considerable publicity. Just as Guilford's AAUP was inspired by the work done at Appalachian State, the work done there was inspired by a growing literature on moral protest techniques.[9]

8. Bauman, Dan. 2020. "Colleges Have Shed a Tenth of Their Employees Since the Pandemic Began," *Chronicle of Higher Education*, November 10, 2020. https://www.chronicle.com/article/colleges-have-shed-a-tenth-of-their-employees-since-the-pandemic-began

9. See, for example: Jasper, James. 1997. *The Art of Moral Protest*, Chicago: University of Chicago Press; McCaughey, Martha and Michael D. Ayers (Eds.), 2003. *Cyberactivism: Online Activism in Theory and Practice*, New York: Routledge; and Diaz-Cepeda, Luis Ruben, and Ernesto Castañeda. 2019. "Activists' Motivations and Typologies: Core Activists in Ciudad Juárez," *Interface* 11:1: 89–122 (July, 2019).

The teach-in: "Who Will Save Guilford College?"

The newly organized and energized AAUP chapter did many things, but none was more important or had a greater influence on subsequent events than the Zoom teach-in that it sponsored on October 21, 2020. By this time the AAUP members, and everyone on the staff and faculty, had seen the writing on the wall, but not many people outside the immediate Guilford community were aware of how drastic things were. The teach-in, titled "Who Will Save Guilford College?", was designed to explain, as much as possible, the college's financial crisis and what had brought it about, the trampling of the processes in the college's handbook that seemed to be taking place, and what might be done to correct the self-destructive course the school was on. Over an hour and a half, various members of the AAUP chapter made presentations on the following topics:

1 What is financial exigency and how do colleges end up in this situation?
2 What is shared governance and why does it matter for academic integrity?
3 Quaker values, shared governance, and difficult times
4 Guilford's allocation of money, treatment of employees, and response to its financial emergency
5 What do students need to know and plan for?

The teach-in was well-publicized in various college communications and on social media, and, lo and behold, 312 people Zoomed in, including current students and faculty, retired faculty, staff, parents, alumni, and even a few members of the board of trustees.

Among those in attendance was Jessie Starling, '00, an associate professor of religious studies at Lewis and Clark College in Portland, OR. Dismayed by what she learned in the teach-in, she immediately began to send direct messages on Facebook to those of her contacts who were Guilford graduates and asked them to spread the word about Guilford's woes. She and another Guilford alum from her era, Jane Murray, '02, then started a Facebook group, choosing the name "Save Guilford College" based on the title of the teach-in. Within a week the group had 1,000 members, and two weeks later it had more than 3,000. A few days after the teach-in, Starling circulated to those who had attended the teach-in as well as her new Facebook friends a draft of a letter to Carol Moore and the Guilford Board of Trustees in which she encouraged them to reconsider the drastic changes being proposed. It included the following plea:

> We recognize that some change is necessary to ensure the college is sustainable during this current inhospitable climate for small liberal arts schools. But the draconian cuts that are currently being considered threaten to destroy the very identity of the school we love. We fear that this new "version" of Guilford will be so academically impoverished that it will have lost its credibility as a true liberal arts institution, and it will fail to attract the necessary number of students to even sustain the debt that recent administrations have incurred.

She sent the letter a few weeks later, by this time with 400 others having signed on, but, as she recalled in an email to me many months later, "Carol [Moore] barged ahead and sent out her termination letters—despite the trustees' assurances to me that they still had time to convene to decide whether to take up her recommendations!"

Using emails and posts on Facebook, the group had already begun to organize. Some Save Guilford College leaders spoke with those who had worked to save other liberal arts colleges that in recent years had faced closing, including Hampshire College, Marlboro College, and Sweet Briar College. They learned from what had worked, and what had not worked, at those schools, and in a series of Zoom meetings attended by a few dozen alumni, they settled into an organizational structure, with a Coordinator or two of each committee as well as liaisons to the Facebook group and the Board of Trustees, faculty, and students:

PR/Communications (communicate Save Guilford College's mission to the community at large, including local and national news outlets, and social media)

Community outreach (educate and engage with the larger Guilford community about what is happening)

Fundraising (build support through a pledge drive to show the board of trustees the breadth of the community ready to financially support Guilford if the college evolves in a direction we as donors feel we can support)

Organization (coordinate among the various committees, ensuring that they are moving in a unified direction with common goals)

Re-envisioning (seek a new direction for the college in line with its values and heritage; this group included four subcommittees that looked at financial matters, recruitment / retention / enrollment, leadership / governance, and how to tell, more effectively, "the Guilford College story")

Legal (consider legal issues related to things happening on campus, and to seek information on establishing 501c3 status for Save Guilford College).

Liaisons (establish board, faculty staff and student liaisons to consult and collaborate with respective shareholders, and to negotiate with respective groups)

Board of trustees accountability (work collaboratively with other committees to try to encourage the board to be more accountable).[10]

As the group explained on its Facebook page:

Save Guilford College is a grassroots movement of alumni and friends of the college. We organized in response to the Guilford chapter of the AAUP's October 2020 teach-in entitled "Who will save Guilford College?" Many of us learned for the first time there about proposals to eliminate nearly half of the college's majors and dozens of tenured faculty in response to an apparently dire financial situation. As beneficiaries of Guilford's radically transformative education, we knew the answer to our professors' question, "Who will save Guilford College?" must be *us*.

Save Guilford College also developed and communicated to the board a list of short-term and long-term demands. Among the short-term demands, for example, was to reject the proposals that Carol Moore put forward to eliminate programs and the accompanying terminations. Among the long-term demands was a call for the college to return to the Quaker-informed shared-governance processes that had always been a hallmark of Guilford.

Money talks

The simple fact that more than 3,000 alumni were involved assured that at least some members of the board were willing

10. Drawn from the slide deck used at the January 2021 community meeting, Save Guilford College (https://www.saveguilfordcollege.com/)

to listen to Save Guilford College (although some seemed to take the view that any bad press from the tough decisions that administrators and boards have to make is inevitable and blows over soon enough). A fund-raising campaign, run by some SGC alumni who had worked professionally as fund-raisers, and who trained other volunteers to make phone calls to prospective donors, certainly got their attention. By January 2021, 850 alumni and friends had pledged to contribute $3.3 million over a five-year period ("if the college evolves in a direction we as donors feel we can support").

Money talks, but so do lawsuits, and even the threat of lawsuits

If holding the teach-in that spawned Save Guilford College was the AAUP chapter's greatest contribution to turning things around, another less apparent contribution was its decision to hire a lawyer to represent the interests of the faculty who had been fired. After first raising some money from members and friends to pay for legal fees, the AAUP chapter then requested and received $1,500 from the NC-AAUP Foundation for "anticipated legal fees." The group held Zoom calls with two lawyers, and hired one of them. It also consulted via Zoom with an expert on legal matters at the national AAUP office in Washington, D. C. The lawyer sent two letters to Carol Moore. The first, sent on October 13, 2020, warned about the process that she was putting in place without the school having declared financial exigency. He wrote:

> This law office represents the Guilford College ("Guilford" or the "College") chapter of the American Association of University Professors (the "Guilford AAUP"). We write to express our client's concerns with the College's plan to eliminate certain academic programs and departments....
>
> Our client's concern stems from the fact that, in tasking the committees with this review, you have invoked

the "finite resources" of the College and the "financial difficulties" the College is facing. We and our client are concerned that you have directed the committees to take into consideration the College's "financial difficulties" as part of its review, even though the College has not declared that a "financial exigency" exists.

In February, he sent another letter. In this three-page letter, he detailed the ways the college had violated its own policies. It included the following: "We and our client feel compelled to note that the Academic Program Prioritization you initiated in September 2020 was an egregious violation of, and deviation from, processes and procedures outlined in the Faculty Handbook (the "Handbook"), which processes and procedures are unequivocally contractual in nature."

Guilford has been sued before, and the trustees probably see lawsuits and the threat of lawsuits as inevitable. Those, however, that generate especially bad publicity (like the one a few years ago, over Title IX violations) lead the college to try hard to settle. In this case, whether or not the AAUP chapter were to win, the publicity generated by a lawsuit claiming that the school fired faculty without having adhered to the Handbook (or its Quaker principles) would not look good. This, along with all the other bad publicity, and the fact that Save Guilford College was attracting money from alumni that might otherwise go directly to the school, led some members, maybe most members, of the board to have second thoughts about the path the school was on.

Set aside?

On January 6, Winslow announced to the community that the board had decided to "set aside" Carol Moore's November 7 proposal, and the terminations she proposed. In a five-paragraph announcement posted on the college's website, he wrote that the trustees were calling for "a time of discernment" and went on to say: "In that spirit, we have asked (interim) President (Carol) Moore to pause implementation of the program prioritization while the board continues to listen and gather input from those of you who wish to offer it. We are hearing particularly from alumni who are offering fundraising ideas."

"Set aside" is a term Quakers use, though not very often. It does not make the online Quaker glossaries that include Quaker favorites like "consensus," "eldering," or "stand aside," so I turned to my favorite Quaker minister. He explained it to me in the following way: "'Set aside' is a term I've seldom heard in Quaker circles, but when used, it's a bit 'gentler' term than 'reject.' It means that there is no sense of the meeting on proceeding with the matter, and it has been set aside until further discernment leads the community to consider it again." As for "discernment," this is Quaker lingo for a process to make decisions by discerning God's will for the community. So, in its vagueness, Winslow's statement, with its use of "set aside" and "discernment," offered no apology, nor was there any clear indication that the November proposals had been rejected—they had been "set aside," and, presumably, after some "discernment," they could be brought back.

A few days before Winslow's "set aside" announcement, the terminated faculty received a terse letter from Carol Moore telling them: "The board has determined to 'pause' the original process to gather additional perspectives on various outcomes of the process. In making this decision, recommendations regarding your position at the college have been put on hold."

On January 6, the day of Winslow's public announcement, they received another, equally terse, and more stilted and legalistic letter, signed by both Carol Moore and Ed Winslow: "Per the recent decision of the Board of Trustees to set aside the program prioritization and proposed faculty terminations, the notice of recommended termination under the program prioritization process has been retracted and any appeals in process are no longer necessary at this time. Any future program or personnel changes will be made in light of developments during the ongoing period of discernment and work." They were still very much in limbo. Those who had entered the job market continued their searches for new employment. Others decided they had better seek alternate work.

During this "time of discernment," the board planned to do two things. First, the school was embarking on an emergency fundraising campaign, "The Guilford Forward Fund," one that would attempt to raise $4 million by May 31, 2021, and another $2 million by January 31, 2022. Second, the board had established four working teams, led by members of the board, made up of trustees, faculty, staff and alumni to identify key milestones related to 1) enrollment stabilization and recruitment; 2) donor challenges and fundraising; 3) faculty and staff collaboration; and 4) constituent engagement.

Another interim president

Six weeks later, on February 23 (ten days after the AAUP lawyer sent his second letter), Winslow informed the Guilford community that Carol Moore was stepping down as interim president (as he put it, "Carol Moore has decided to conclude her time with the College, originally planned for June") and that Jim Hood had agreed to serve as interim president. Jim Hood—the very person I had recommended to Winslow in the email I sent him eight months earlier—as I noted to Winslow, and noted above, is a Guilford alumnus, a long-time member of the English department, a recent clerk of the faculty, and a birthright Quaker. Those throughout the Guilford community, including those active with AAUP and Save Guilford College, were not unhappy to see that Moore was leaving (that is putting it mildly) and were encouraged by the choice of Jim Hood to replace her.

The college's emergency fund-raising campaign went well, and reached the goal of $4 million by May 31. The fund-raising committee for Save Guilford College had embarked on a phone-calling effort to persuade those who had previously pledged money (the $3.3 million over five years) now to pony up. Soon the group had $300,000 in a special account it had set up, separate from the college. As a gesture of support for some of the changes that the board had made (not implementing the program prioritization recommendations, and replacing Carol Moore with Jim Hood), while still acknowledging that there were many issues on the group's short-term and long-term lists that had yet to be addressed, SGC released a $25,000 gift on April 6 (the Advancement Office's official "Day for Guilford") and then toward the end of May an additional $250,000, the largest gift the college received in this phase of its Guilford Forward Campaign. (Wisely, in early May, 2021, when Guilford announced its annual alumni awards, it honored SGC by giving it the "outstanding volunteer award").

Once Jim Hood was in office, various cost-saving efforts were put into place as the school planned for the 2021-22 budget. Many had been on the lists of ideas that the curriculum committee and the clerk's committee had submitted to Carol Moore back in October. Some faculty took an early retirement option. Others took voluntary unpaid leaves. Yet others chose to reduce their teaching load, and their salary, to two-thirds. As Jim Hood reported in a message to the community, about $1 million had been cut from the payroll because ten tenured faculty members had resigned, four more had retired, four were taking a year of unpaid leave, and nine had agreed to take pay cuts in exchange for reduced workloads. As he explained, contrasting his approach with that of the previous interim president, "We have gotten those savings through a voluntary program instead of by imposition. It was done in a collaborative manner, and that's a really great accomplishment."

Jim also provided the long-missing institutional acknowledgment that things had been mishandled, and he made clear, in writing, to those who had received termination letters that their employment was "fully reinstated." In a letter sent in early April to the faculty who had been terminated (all of whom he knew personally), he wrote:

> Understanding how professionally and emotionally taxing this entire ordeal was, now in my role as Interim President, I wish to communicate the following things....
>
> ....I have communicated to other faculty my agreement with the findings of the faculty Appeals Boards that did continue that the termination process did not adhere to the guidelines set out by the Guilford College Faculty Handbook....
>
> Finally, I want you to know that your employment with Guilford College is fully reinstated under the terms set forth in your letter of agreement for the academic year 2021-22, which is forthcoming from the Interim Provost.

The budget approved for the 2021-2022 academic year had a surplus of about $1.3 million, but that was only possible because of about $7 million that came in from various programs, especially in loan forgiveness money from the federal government as part of the Biden administration's Payback Protection Program (PPP). The next budget, for 2022-23, is likely to pose major challenges, especially if enrollment does not improve.

When Jim Hood was hired to serve as an interim president, plans were already in place for a presidential search, this one led by AGB Search, a different firm from the one that specializes in interim searches used in May 2020 to hire Carol Moore. Two members of the board, both alumni, were co-chairs of the search committee. They, and the chair of the board, said on more than one occasion that they hoped to have a new president in place by August. Hood made it clear that he was not a candidate, though he was willing to stay on past August if need be. Many hoped the board would not make their final decisions during the summer, when no students and few faculty were around, but would wait until the fall semester began so there could be community input.

The co-chairs of the search committee reported in mid-August, just as school was about to begin, that 79 people had applied to be the next president, the larger Advisory Group (25 people) had narrowed the 79 down to nine, and the smaller Selection Committee (12 people) had recommended four of the nine to the board of trustees. The board planned to interview those four, and then, as the co-chairs explained, it would "decide which candidates to invite for campus visits and meetings with members of the college community."

So, the 2021-22 academic year began with Jim Hood still the interim president, with a new provost (Maria Rosales, Professor of Political Science, who had just completed her first year as clerk of the faculty, chosen by Jim Hood with considerable input from the faculty), most of the Fernandes Cabinet having departed, and the Guilford community awaiting the appointment of a new president. Students were back on campus, and most classes were scheduled to take place in person. The delta variant of the coronavirus, however, was surging, nationally and in North Carolina, so COVID uncertainty was again on the rise.

Conclusions

Over the next decade, many schools will close, and Guilford may be one of them. Major changes in the way faculty and staff are treated, effective leadership from the new president and that person's senior administrators, and successful promotion of the school leading to higher enrollment—all of these are needed for long-term survival.

Yet another area of improvement will be necessary if Guilford is to survive: more effective leadership and greater transparency from the board of trustees. In a typical straightforward and hard-hitting letter sent in July 2021 to the interim president, the newly hired interim chief financial officer, and members of the board, calling for greater transparency about financial matters past, present, and future, Save Guilford College identified the crucial importance of more effective leadership from the board:

> The hard truth is that Guilford College, as a four-year, Quaker-rooted liberal arts college may not be viable beyond the next few years. The reasons for the college's recent decline and current crisis are not rooted primarily in market forces, nor in the exigencies of the pandemic. They are rooted in the board's failure with regards to its two primary legal responsibilities: (a) safeguarding the endowment and (b) hiring and firing the president.
>
> These are the primary reasons why the faculty overwhelmingly voted "No Confidence" in board leadership last November, a historic occurrence that the board still has not publicly responded to.

Even if the future of the college is not "viable beyond the next few years," many faculty whose jobs were terminated still have those jobs, at least for the foreseeable future, many on the board have been willing participants in discussions about how things need to change, and the school has bought some time and thus a fighting chance to survive intact. A June 2021 article in *The Triad Business Journal* was accurately titled "Can Guilford

College Survive? Confidence Builds, but Questions Linger." [11] Another article, in late July 2021, this one in Greensboro's local newspaper, the *News & Record*, was titled "Is Guilford College on Track to Recovery? Yes and No." In it, the author argued that "as long as Guilford continues to gloss over failed leadership," and here he focused on the board and especially the chair of the board, the substantive needed changes will not occur. [12]

So, my first year of retirement, 2020-21, was an academic year in which the school had three presidents (two of whom were interim), the double whammy of a serious debt crisis coupled with the coronavirus, academic programs that were scheduled to be eliminated but then weren't, faculty who were terminated and then reinstated, many faculty who had decided to retire early or who had accepted jobs at other schools, and classes held online. Still, there were encouraging signs for the coming academic year, 2021-2022. Because of the trusted leadership of Jim Hood, the appointment of Maria Rosales as provost, and the efforts of the board to be more inclusive and transparent, a case could be made for cautious optimism. However, as I have indicated, there is also much to worry about when it comes to the long-term viability of the school.

In May, the AAUP chapter held its last Zoom meeting of the academic year. The group selected officers for the coming year, thanked one another (profusely) for the invaluable

11. Warren, Trajan. 2021. "Can Guilford College survive? Confidence builds, but questions linger," *Triad Business Journal*, June 25, 2021. https://www.bizjournals.com/triad/news/2021/06/25/can-guilford-college-survive.html

12. Podolsky, Jonathon. 2021. "Is Guilford College on track to recovery? Yes…and no." *News & Record*, July 25, 2021. https://greensboro.com/opinion/columnists/jonathon-podolsky-is-guilford-college-on-track-to-recovery-yes-and-no/article_26ecd736-e4b2-11eb-9627-bb4a32e4762a.html

emotional and professional support they had given to each other throughout a very stressful time, and said farewell to those members who had decided either to retire early or to leave for jobs at other schools (three of the four AAUP officers would not be back in the fall). One person lamented that the AAUP chapter still was seen by some in the Guilford community, including some (perhaps many) members of the board, as a group of disgruntled academics and she noted, wistfully, that the group had gotten little credit for the valuable role it had played. I responded that I was convinced that if it had not been for the AAUP, especially the teach-in and the threats of a lawsuit, Guilford would not have brought a halt to the dreadful path it was on, one that seemed destined either to bring the school down or to save it in a way that was going to be unrecognizable as the liberal arts college it once was. Based on that conversation, I concluded that the story of the valuable role the chapter played should be told, not only to give credit to those who worked so hard to save the soul of the college, but to encourage others, at other schools, when faced with what looks like impending doom, that activism can work.

Part Two

Geezerball

North Carolina Basketball at its Eldest

(Sort of a Memoir)

For Claire—
founding member of The Committee Meeting,
longtime participant in the Geezer Game,
valued colleague, and treasured friend

We do not quit playing because we grow old.
We grow old because we quit playing.

GEORGE BERNARD SHAW

I *Call Me Commish*

CALL ME COMMISH. Some people do. I'm the organizer of a pickup basketball game that started in 1976, perhaps the longest running pickup game in North Carolina, or maybe even the nation. Who knows? A small group of us started playing, half-court, in 1976, in what is now called the old gym at Guilford College, the Quaker-affiliated school where I have been teaching since 1974. Just a few years before we started our game, future NBA players M. L. Carr and Lloyd Free (later known as World B. Free) had led the college's men's basketball team to the NAIA title, in that same gym, known as "The Crackerbox." It was the setting for many a basketball thrill.

My first year at Guilford was Lloyd Free's third and final year. He averaged 25.4 points per game, the team went 24-4, he was the NAIA player of the year, and he was drafted by Philadelphia in the second round of the NBA draft. Watching games that year in the Crackerbox (capacity: 933), crammed in as we were like the spectators at Indiana high school gyms portrayed in the movie *Hoosiers*, was the most exciting basketball I have ever seen.[1]

I grew up in an era when those of us who were athletic played many sports. In the summer we played softball or baseball, we swam, we played golf and we played tennis. In the fall we played touch football (sometimes in the street). In the winter we played basketball. This was long before kids were encouraged or pressured to choose a particular sport. I was not a great athlete, but I played on my junior high school basketball and softball teams, and I played baseball and wrestled in high school. I liked basketball, but I was short (still am), and certainly had no sense that it would later become such a central part of my life.

From the time I was young, I liked racquet sports. My family had a much-used ping pong table in our house, and during the summers, especially at the overnight camp I attended from the time I was seven until I was 19, and then as a counselor for two years, I played a lot of tennis. In college, I learned to play squash. In California in the early 1970s, when one of my graduate school friends introduced me to racquetball, I fell in love with it. By the time I came to North Carolina in 1974 to teach at Guilford, I was playing racquetball four or five times a week. One of the first things I did after we moved to Greensboro was to scout out the local racquetball courts, and I soon found some guys to play with. For the first few years, I played about three times a week, and played in some local tournaments. I came in second in the city tournament in 1976, my racquetball peak.

1. The 933 figure is from Herb Appenzeller, *Pride in the Past*, published by Guilford College, 1987, p. 173. According to Appenzeller, the fire marshal set the capacity, and the basketball crowds in the Crackerbox were so large that a person was placed at the door with a clicker to count people off and to stop people from entering once capacity was reached.

When the small group of faculty and students began to play pick-up basketball in the Crackerbox we played just once a week. Soon we were playing twice a week, and, after a while, three times a week. Although I was a better racquetball player than basketball player, I enjoyed the basketball more—the game was more social, it called for more teamwork and strategy, and the interpersonal interactions were more complex. Eventually I was playing a lot of basketball and almost no racquetball.

More and more students and faculty joined the game. We had brief, sometimes very brief, appearances from other faculty, perhaps the original "one and done" players. A few administrators even showed up to play once or twice, but none lasted long. Bruce Stewart was one administrator who made a cameo appearance. Bruce left Guilford to become the Headmaster at Abington Friends and, from 1998 through 2009 he was the Headmaster at Sidwell Friends in Washington, D. C. He became a member of the Guilford College Board of Trustees in 1986, and the Chair of the Board from 1999 through 2003. He is the only member of the Board of Trustees ever to play in our game, though we extended an invitation to M. L. Carr, who was on campus periodically while he was on the Board from 1998 through 2009. At one point one of the guys in our game sent a letter inviting Barack Obama to play any time he came to North Carolina.

In the early days, we called our game "The Committee Meeting." This allowed us to avoid other mid-day commitments (for example, attempts by any of the committees I was on, such as the Curriculum Committee, to schedule a lunch meeting on a Monday, Wednesday or Friday). This ruse did not last for long, as everyone on campus soon knew of our dissembling—we even entered a team by that name in the college's intramural league. Decades later, I'm not sure when, I began jokingly to call it "The Geezer Game." Even though a few of the younger studs (relatively speaking of course) were offended by this term, it stuck.

This first era, from 1976 through 1981, for the most part a faculty-student half-court-game, ended when the college built the Ragan-Brown Field House in 1981. This kicked off a second era, during which the college began a twenty-year affiliation with the YMCA—the Y paid the college some amount of money, and Y members, including a coterie of basketball players, were allowed to use the facility. As the game moved from the Crackerbox to Ragan-Brown, gradually the number of those playing increased, and at some point we shifted from half-court to full-court. By the mid-1980s there were more non-Guilfordians playing noontime hoops than Guilford employees or students. By 2001 or so, there were enough players that we often had two, and sometimes three, full-court games running simultaneously. Over time, the games became more and more physical, not unlike the run-and-gun games you might find at any Y. To preserve the nature of our game—which historically had been competitive but less physical and less territorial than most pickup games—those of us from the college and those Y guys who preferred our "style" of basketball began to arrive early and we began to start our game on the most distant court from the entryway (court #3).

As a result, what had been a noon-time game gradually began at 11:45, and then, because more and more people came early, at 11:30. This meant that our game already had started when many of the bigger, faster, and mostly younger run-and-gun guys arrived. They would start a new game on court #1, and, as noted, some days there were enough players to start a third game on the middle court (court #2).

In November 2000, near the end of this second era, one of our regular players, Craig Chappelow, who worked for the Center for Creative Leadership, wrote an article about our game in which he described the participants in the following way: "The group is a hodgepodge of former jocks and nonathletes from all professions. Last week my teammates consisted of an engineer, a podiatrist, an artist, and a guy who collects tractors."[2]

A key turning point took place in 2002 when a new branch of the YMCA, the Alex W. Spears III Family YMCA[3], was built just a few miles away, and the college and the Y terminated their agreement. The Y members were told that they would no longer be able to use the college facilities, and they were encouraged to join the Spears YMCA. Some already had citywide Y memberships that allowed them to play at Spears, and others were willing to join Spears. However, many of the Y members who played regularly in our game (down on court #3) knew that we had something special, something that they were unlikely to find or recreate at the Y. They very much wanted to continue to play at Guilford, and those of us employed by Guilford who played in the game wanted them to be able to do so.

This, I now think, is when I began to take on the quasi-official role of Commissioner. I approached Brian Wenger, the

2. Chappelow, Craig. 2000. "Order on the Court: A Lesson in Leadership." *Leadership in Action* 20(5):14.

3. Alexander W. Spears, III, was the CEO of Lorillard Tobacco Company from 1995 until 1999. He died of lung cancer in 2001. After Spears' death, the obituary in the local Greensboro paper was laudatory, even hagiographic, but the obituary in the *New York Times*, which emphasized his "unapologetic" claims that nicotine was not addictive and that "it has not been scientifically proven that smoking causes illness in humans," presented him in a far less favorable light. I recommend the 2016 documentary film, "Obit," about the obituary writers at the *New York Times*. The sometimes subtle but clearly political nature of obituaries is more widespread than many people realize, as I explored in an article in 2004 titled "Making Rags Out of Riches: Horatio Alger and the Tycoon's Obituary," in *Extra! The Magazine of FAIR—the Media Watch Group*, 17 (1):27-28.

guy who was then in charge of the facility, he directed me to the person he reported to in the administrative hierarchy, and he in turn sent the request further up the line. No one was sure whether the non-Guilford employees should be allowed to continue to play at Guilford, or under what conditions. One main concern was liability, but another was whether they should pay, and, how much. Finally, I was told, it got to the college's then relatively new President, Kent Chabotar, and, in a very wise move on his part, he allegedly (I was not there) said, "Sure, let them keep playing."[4] The deal that ultimately was reached was that I, like one of the coaches, could "rent" the court for three hours a week, at the discount rate of $27 per hour that the coaches paid for the various camps that they ran, especially during the summer. Thus, for $81 a week, or, about $4,000 a year, we could rent the court.

Although some players arrived by 11:30, the game usually began by 11:45, and we typically played until about 1, it was

4. I have no doubt that by the time Kent Chabotar stepped down from the presidency in 2014, I was perceived by some as one of his more outspoken critics. Although I thought he was quite capable when it came to some aspects of his job, I did at times publically criticize certain actions that he and his administration took. For example, when the college, with minimal faculty input, and certainly without faculty approval, accepted a ten-year grant from the BB&T Foundation that stipulated that some students would be required to read Ayn Rand's *Atlas Shrugged*, the lengthy polemical novel that has taken on biblical dimensions for some right-wing thinkers, a book that endorses individualism, justifies selfishness, and idealizes capitalism, I wrote an article in 2010 that was published in *Academe* titled "Is This Curriculum for Sale?" Despite such public criticisms, I believe that Kent had clear strengths, and some very good moments—his decision to allow the off-campus geezers the ability to continue playing in the midday game was one of his best (though he might not place it near the top of his list).

agreed that we could pay for only one hour per day, three times a week. No one has questioned this. In fact, during some periods in the 17 years since this system went into effect (especially periods of extensive administrative turn-over), I'm not sure if anyone would have noticed if I stopped paying completely.

Therefore, in an email to the non-Guilfordians I explained that if they paid me what was likely to be about $300 per year (much less than the cost of joining Spears) that we should have enough money to cover the rental of the court; I did not ask those employed by the college to pay anything on the grounds that access to the field house was a perquisite that came with their employment (see Appendix 5 for that email explaining our options; it also includes a list of those who received the email, the "charter members" of the post-2003 game).

This was the start of the third era (what might be considered our "modern era"). Now, 16 years later, we are still renting the court (same cost—no inflation yet), and so this now 27-year-old game got past this institutional hurdle in 2003. We pay $810 every ten weeks. The college provides a court, shower facilities, and most years, towels (some years we have had to bring our own). It has from my point of view definitely been a win-win.

There have been ups and downs, smooth and not so smooth periods, some new players who fit in nicely to the game, and some who have not fit in so well. There have been many rule changes proposed, and some adopted; there have been arguments, with players walking off the court in anger; and there even have been fights. For the most part, the game has endured with relatively few major problems. We are definitely older, and maybe wiser.

How is it that this pickup game has lasted more than 40 years? What have we done that has allowed for such longevity? There are I am sure many factors at play, but I think that three guiding principles have been especially important. The first is that everyone gets to play an equal amount. The second is that we try our best to keep injuries and arguments to a minimum. And the third is based on the slogan that the Chinese used during the Cold War: "Friendship First, Competition Second." This slogan became known to Americans when, after more than twenty years during which the two countries had neither diplomatic nor economic relations, an American table tennis team was invited to visit Communist China in 1971. My wife, Lisa, still says "friendship first" to me when I leave the house to play ball.

2 *Entering the Geezerhood*

MUCH AS I RESPECT democratic voting procedures, and the value of consensus (especially here in Quakerland), in the geezer game we rarely take votes and we typically don't achieve consensus in the traditional Quaker way. (I'll note, parenthetically, that having worked at a Quaker-affiliated college for more than four decades, "achieving consensus in the traditional Quaker way" is not as clear-cut a concept as it might sound).

In that initial email that I sent to 30 players, back in June 2003 (see Appendix 5),[1] I laid out my willingness to oversee

1. Nine of the 30 recipients of that email are still playing: Craig Chappelow, Thom Espinola, Rusty Hoffman, Ron Irons, Charlie Johnson, Dan Lenze, Danny McCoy, Steve Schlehuser, Bob Williams, and me. Two are on the extended disabled list but allege that they are coming back (Rob Luisana and Bob Wineburg). One has a new job and has been unable to play for most of the last six months, but shows up periodically, and is still therefore part of the geezerhood (Greg Mayer). At least three have died (thankfully, not on the court): George Cox, Robert Pearse, and Darryl Rolandelli.

the game but my unwillingness to try to run a parliamentary or traditional Quaker meeting. I wrote the following:

> I'm sure that there will be decisions to make along the way about membership and other matters. My plan is to make these decisions myself, unless I want or need help. If I do, then I will draw on a Guilford College Interdisciplinary Basketball-Playing Faculty Kitchen Cabinet consisting of Thom Espinola (physics), Claire Morse (psychology) and Bob Williams (economics). In addition, I'm assuming that at times, I'll poll all paying members (to decide, for example, whether to include a new person in the game, or, just to come up with a wild example, whether to ban someone who makes the mistake of starting a fight or throwing the ball in someone's face).

Over the many years of the game, we have, of course, lost players. Some have moved away, some have changed jobs and no longer can play midday, some have what we think of as "career-ending injuries," and, as I have noted (well, footnoted), a few have died.

So, too, have we added players. Typically, someone has heard about the game, one of our current players has a friend or a colleague who is interested in playing, or the college has hired a new employee who wants to play. When this happens, I ask the potential new player to call or email me, I arrange to meet with them (often over coffee or beer), I explain the game to them, including the rules we use, the culture of the game, and the costs for those not employed by Guilford. For many years we had a Sunday game at a local high school, and we had the option of trying people out in that game before making a commitment to allow them in our game, but the Sunday game has faded (long story).

For the most part we have operated on the assumption that the game is for older, not younger, players, though over the years we have moved the cut-off point upwards. Mostly I recall saying that we should not allow anyone to join the game who is under 40 and, if we make exceptions, they have to promise to pass the ball and play defense. Right now, among the active players, the oldest is 78, and the youngest is 39. The average age is 61.7: in addition to the one guy still in his late thirties, three are in their 40s, six in their 50s, seven in their 60s, and four in their 70s. (The Commissioner is 74). Of course, by the time you read this, if all goes well, we all will be older.

Currently all of the geezers are male. Claire Morse, my wonderful colleague in the psychology department for many years, played in the game from its inception in 1976 until she retired from teaching, and from the geezer game, in 2011. Other women periodically have played in the game, including, at times, members of Guilford's women's basketball team during their off-season. In an article that she wrote in 1985 about "The Committee Meeting," Claire concluded: "These men are comrades of a special sort, and our shared play can certainly lead me to respect and enjoy them from the perspective of a woman who has been allowed to participate simply as another player in a game we all enjoy."[2]

Here is what might be a typical example of how we decided to let a guy in the game. It took place back in 2006, when we were still trying to figure out what procedure to follow. Rob Luisana, the owner of an insurance agency who began to play in our game in the late 1980s, wrote an article for the local paper about a group of our geezers who had participated in a three-on-three tournament at East Carolina University, part of the North Carolina Senior Games. Not long after that, Mike

2. Morse, Claire. 1985. "The Committee Meeting: Guilford's Noontime Basketball." *Guilford Review* 22(Fall):19.; see Appendix 6A.

R., a guy who read the article, showed up at the Guilford gym to watch us play. He talked with one of our players, Bob Wineburg, who wrote me about him ("He is 6' 5" and seems nice. He hasn't played in a year and would like to know what the procedure is to get in the game."). Bob gave me the guy's email, I wrote him, and we arranged to meet for coffee. I liked him, and thought he'd be a nice addition to the game, so I sent an email to the geezers, asking their approval. After numerous humorous emails (one wrote, "Don't forget the criminal background check," another wrote, "I vote yes... but prefer to run his credit and get a financial statement!!!," and a third wrote, "Since I'd love for someone else to cover Ron, I vote 'yea'"), Craig Chappelow wrote a longer, (mostly) more serious, reply. It included the following:

> OK, you guys have had your fun. The commissioner has asked for your serious input, which he didn't have to do, and he gets some kind of comedy routine back in return. I think the only way to do this is to let the new guy "naked walk" down the hall to the shower. If Guilford receives any student complaints about lumps, scars, or body hair—he's in!
>
> OK, serious answer. I think the question is as much about a process for considering new folks as it is about this Mike guy. Some alternatives below. I could live with any of them, but my preference would be the first.
>
> 1. Let the numbers drive openings for new people. Right now the numbers are great—always enough, seldom too many. If adding new people means I would end up on half court more, I'd vote no. But if a regular were to leave, then we would add to balance the numbers.
>
> 2. Let Richie decide. He knows what we're looking for and could probably get a sense quick enough. Downside

is if the guy turns out to be a Biff [a former player from the pre-Spears days, big trouble], I would also be looking to Richie to deal with the problem.

3. Let the guy play free for a few days and then have some quick discussion and decision among the regulars.

Open to any other suggestions. No more engineers please.

We let him play. He was a nice addition. Unfortunately, after playing only four times, he wrote to tell me that his back was giving him too much trouble, and he could no longer play ("I am going to have stop with the basketball. The back can't just handle it—the problems are different but in the same area.").

This pretty much set the pattern as various people have asked to join the game over the years. Some, like Mike R., only played a few times before disappearing for one reason or another. Others we let in the game and they have become regular participants. Some we decided against.

A trickier or at least different issue has emerged as people who work at the college have asked about joining us. I have argued that we should include them, in part because I believe that for the game to endure we need the support of administration and staff. This has meant that even though some of those who have asked to play have been younger than 40, or didn't exactly play the game we like (that is, they played a more physical game or a more run-and-gun game, they were less likely to pass the ball, and less likely to play defense), we have in every case said yes. For example, at one point, a staff member who had been playing in the game for a while (Rex), asked if his boss (Jon) could join the game.

Here is what I wrote to the geezers about this request:

Geezers,

Rex mentioned to me last Wednesday that his boss...whose official title is something like Associate Vice President of Operations and Facilities, has expressed interest in playing with us in the noontime game. I told Rex that I was going out of town, and that I would contact Jon when I got back. I want to touch base with you first.

I'm ambivalent, but lean toward letting him in. He was supportive when I first approached the administration about us renting the gym (though, ultimately, it was the support of Kent Chabotar, the President, that settled the matter). In no small part because he is in charge of all facilities on campus, I think the long-term health of the game might be enhanced by allowing him to play (and it might not be enhanced if we don't let him to play, though that may not be the case).

[Jon] looks to be about 40 or so, maybe a bit older, and I have not seen him play...I think it is the right thing to do to allow not just full-time faculty but also full-time staff to play in the game—we faculty already have many privileges compared to many others who work at the college, and I am uncomfortable saying that faculty can play but staff cannot.

Let me know what you think. I plan to contact Jon within a day or two.

RICHIE

We let Jon in, and he played for a number of years until his sudden departure from the college (about which the rumors are still flying). Although some of the big guys who had to cover him might not agree with me, I think he was a net plus, in no small part because he let us into the gym on days when the college was officially closed, and apparently he was instrumental in arranging to have a court named after me when I turned 70 (more on that to come).

So, too, did I approach the geezerhood about another staff member, Mark, who at the time he asked to join the game was only 35 years old. Here is the email I wrote to them before we let him in the game:

Geezers,

We have a request to join the game from Mark..., who has been a full-time employee at Guilford College for the past two months (he is the Interim Director of ITS). He heard about the game (Rex), emailed me about playing, and I met with him today. I explained to him the history of the Geezer Game (the short version—10 minutes or so), and some of the rules that have evolved over the years (e.g., Half Court Monday—I didn't include the history of whether to call backcourt or not, or how we deal with balls that hit the wire above the backboard). I emphasized that we try to avoid conflicts, both physical and verbal, and that we have various strategies to do so (e.g., not having to win to stay on the court, calling jump balls instead of trying to resolve disagreements). He seemed to understand.

One possible glitch is that he is younger than 40—he is only 36. He assures me that he is out of shape and feels older. He was sitting down, so I am not sure how tall he is, but I could see that he is not a point guard and that he has a pretty good size spare tire on him. He did not play high school or college ball, but has played pickup, industrial league, and he has coached both children and teenagers. Just from looking at him, I'd say that if I had to assign him someone to cover, I'd have him cover Steve the Really Elder or Danny (not Andy, Chris, Bob Williams, Tim, or Thom). He has not played in the last six months. I suggested to him that if we let him play, he begin with Half Court Monday, though I informed him that we had not played full court in a while.

I explained to him that permission would be needed from the geezerhood, and that I would get back to him after I had emailed you. I recommend that we let him in, despite his youth. Among other things, my department and I depend greatly on computers, and I need to maintain good relations with those who work in ITS.

Please let me know if you have objections. If I don't hear any within a few days, I'll invite him to join us one of these Mondays...

RICHIE

So, that is our system, such as it is. I consult with the geezerhood, but ultimately I decide (participatory autocracy?). For the most part this has worked.

How Much Do They Pay To Play?

AS I HAVE INDICATED, since 2003 we have been renting the court, and the fee from the college has not changed, nor has the fee for the geezers increased until recently. The payment system I have put in place is that the geezers pay me, either the full fee for the entire year, with a discount (the optimists) or two payments due in January and July, for the first and second six months of the year (the pessimists). Until recently, the optimists were given a slight discount (and paid $275) and the pessimists made two payments of $150. Because we recently had a drop in our numbers (due to injuries and a few people changing to new jobs that interfered with their basketball schedule), I increased the annual fee from $300 to $350—the optimists who paid for the entire year still received a discount, and paid only $300, and the pessimists paid two installments of $175.

Inevitably, adjustments needed to be made when guys got hurt and were out for long periods of time or had new jobs that allowed them only to play once in a while, or, in a few cases, only played in the summer. I have allowed part-time participants to play for $5 per day, using an honor system— they keep track, and at the end of the year they pay me whatever the total comes to. For example, the college houses the Eastern Music Festival every summer. For a few years, Calvin J., one of the administrators in that program, who came to Greensboro from his home in Florida for six weeks or so, saw us playing and asked if he could join us. We let him play, and I arranged for him to pay $5 for each day that he played (as a result, we pulled in $30 in 2006, and $25 in 2007). So, too, with Steve H., an alum who played regularly in our game when he was a student and continued to play for a number of years after he graduated while he still lived in Greensboro. He now lives in Maryland, but he shows up every few summers, and plays for a week or two. Another guy, Cliff M., accumulates so much leave time where he works that late in the calendar year he has to take some days off or lose them; for the last few years, he has been able to play 10-12 times, almost always on Fridays in November and December, and sometimes during the year on holidays when the company he works for is closed but the college is open. Tim M. played for about a year, and then moved to Hawaii, but during the summer when he visits family in Greensboro he plays in the game. The fact that these players return when they are in town or come back to play when their work schedules allow, speaks to the long-term appeal of the game—people hate to give it up, just as the regulars hate to miss playing on the days that they can't. Though at the time of the 2019 increase from $300 to $350 one geezer raised questions about whether Guilford employees should have to pay to play, and about whether the $5 system for those who could not play often was fair to those who paid full freight, this system has mostly gone without challenge or problems.

I have an excel file which shows who paid, how much they paid, and the date on which they paid. It allows me to keep track of "delinquents," those who are more than a few weeks late in their payments—I send them reminder emails when necessary. I keep the money in an account at my bank, and I write checks to Guilford College every ten weeks for $810. Each year, we have had a little left over, and some years we have given Christmas gifts to the administrator in charge of the facility. One year we bought a fancy digital clock for the college and, under it, on the wall next to the court that we usually play on, we arranged for a plaque that says it was given to the college by the geezers. The plaque includes the following quote by George Bernard Shaw: "We do not quit playing because we grow old. We grow old because we quit playing."

3   *Participatory Autocracy*

WHEN IT COMES to figuring out the rules we play by, I have used this same somewhat autocratic approach that draws on consultation and sometimes even achieves consensus. When I told one of the geezers that I was writing about how the game had lasted so long, and I mentioned the phrase, "participatory autocracy," he reminded me that Bruce Springsteen made a similar decision early in the life of the E Street Band—Bruce told the others in the band that he wanted input from them, but ultimately he was going to make the key decisions about the music, about the performances, and about the marketing. Bruce's power over the lives of those in the E Street Band was much greater than whatever influence I have had over the geezers, and, accordingly, whereas I use the phrase "participatory autocracy" he uses the phrase "benevolent dictatorship." Here is part of how he explained his role with the band: "I didn't want to get into any more decision making squabbles or have any confusion about who set the creative direction of my music....I look back on this as being one of the smartest decisions of my young life....I crafted a benevolent dictatorship: creative input was welcome within the structure I prepared..."[1] I am not sure that this is the best way to go about keeping a pickup basketball game going, or that all groups would accept participatory autocracy, but this has worked pretty well for us (and the benevolent dictatorship has worked for Bruce and the E Street Band).

Winners Up?

ONE OF OUR guiding principles has been that everyone should get to play, and another has been that we should strive to reduce the deleterious effects of territoriality. On many courts the prevailing system is "winners up." That is, when there are extra players, the first one to arrive who is not in the game calls next game ("I got next"), and that person forms a team (sometimes simply by choosing teammates from the players on the team that lost and any others waiting to play, sometimes based simply on who is waiting and the order in which they arrived, sometimes based on shooting foul shots). The team that won the previous game stays on the court. This, of course, puts an even greater premium on winning. I have no doubt that arguments are more likely to occur and fights are more likely to break out when people are playing to keep the court. Moreover, no one wants to have to sit and watch others play (especially in a noon-time game when many have to get back to work). Though newcomers sometimes suggest it, we never have played winners up.

Therefore, the system we use is that with an even number of players (6, 8, or 10), we simply make teams and play, trying, as best we can, to make even teams so the games will be close. Typically, I make the teams. If I am late, or if I am not there, someone else does. In his November 2000 article about the

1. Springsteen, Bruce. 2016. *Born to Run*. New York: Simon and Schuster.

game, Craig Chappelow wrote the following: "Everyone looks to Richie to divide the players into teams to get the games started—not because the rest of us can't but because Richie has an uncanny knack for setting up balanced teams. Dan McCoy, a mortgage banker and lunch league regular, points out that 'Richie would enjoy nothing more than a three-game split with the scores 15 to 13."[2] Danny McCoy was right: I do want close games. My ideal day has the two teams splitting the first two games (both of which are close), with the third game decided when I hit the game-winning shot, preferably a three.

If we have an odd number, say 7, 9 or 11, one team gets an extra player, and that team rotates that player in and another player out every 10 points. If we have 12 players, each team has six, and the two teams each rotate a player out every 10 points (usually two people who are guarding each other go out together, though this does not always work based on when people have arrived); if we have 13 players, then one team has 7, the other 6, and every 10 points the seven-person team rotates two people out, while the six-person team rotates one person out. This is one of the cases when we have had on-court votes. With 13, there is the question of whether to play one five-on-five game (rotating three people in and out) or two three-on-three games (with a sub in one of the games). Some of us (this includes me), following the principle that no one wants to sit, have argued for two games; others, who hate to play three-on-three, prefer the five-on-five game with a three-person rotation. For a while we voted, but after three votes in a row in which the group chose to play one game, not two, we stopped taking votes at 13 (though there are still, periodically, calls for a vote, and some geezers might be shifting in their view on this).

2. Chappelow, Craig. 2000. "Order on the Court: A Lesson in Leadership." *Leadership in Action* 20(5):15.

With the arrival of a 14th person, we used to just split into two games, sometimes asking the latest arrivals to play in the three-on-three game, not the four-on-four game. Again, some people balked, and in fact, one guy left the gym in anger one day rather than be demoted to the three-on-three game (the three-on-three game has at times been referred to as the "J. V. game"). For a period, we voted whether to play one or two games when we had 14, but the voting process was surprisingly laborious (some people abstained, some half raised their hands), and resistance remained. The policy that has evolved for the time being at least is that I ask if six people are willing to play three-on-three (me and five others). If so, those volunteers head to the other end of the court and play three-on-three, leaving the remaining eight to play four-on-four (if another person arrives, #15, that person rotates into the larger game; if #16 arrives, we have two four-on-four games). This is as good an example as any of the realization that my above-mentioned "somewhat autocratic approach" is only "somewhat"—one can only ignore the wishes of the people to a certain extent or rebellion takes place.

One more thing to negotiate is when to add players into an ongoing game. Many of those in our game come to play during their lunch hours, and their work responsibilities mean that some people drift in shortly or well after we have started the first (or even the second) game. Some always arrive early. Some are chronically late. One player, let's call him John Smith, always comes late so he is generally referred to as "the late John Smith." If we have just started, or if we are midway through the game, no problem, we add late arrivals. If, however, we are close to the end of the game, especially if it is a close game, we sometimes make the latecomer wait until the game ends. It is yet another subjective decision, one that sometimes I make, and sometimes is made by a quick effort at on-court consensus.

Make it Take it?

SIMILARLY, MANY, MAYBE most, pickup games go by what is called "make it, take it," which means that (unlike real games, with officials and clocks) after a basket is made the team that just scored gets the ball again. This allows the stronger team to win the game quickly, conceivably without the losing team ever getting the ball. In an attempt to avoid lopsided games, we have never played "make it, take it."

How Many Points Per Game?

FOR MANY YEARS, we played games to 15, each basket counting as one point, but you had to win by two (which led to some memorable overtime games that went well into the high 20s, maybe even the low 30s). In 2006, a subgroup began to play in The Senior Games, an annual three-on-three tournament held at East Carolina University, and in that tournament they used the three-point line. The first year we played, we realized that they scored the way most high schools, colleges, and the pros did: regular baskets counted as two points, shots from behind the three-point line as three points, and foul shots as one point. In 2007, for a month or so prior to going back to ECU for a second year, we began to use the three-point line at Guilford to practice our outside shots and to prepare for the tournament's scoring system. We changed the scoring system from games to 15, with each basket counting one point, to games to 30, with threes counting three and other baskets counting two (we don't shoot foul shots). People seemed to like this, maybe in part because it mirrored "real" basketball, so we have stuck with it. We did not keep the win-by-two rule, so we no longer have the possibility of overtime games.

Full Court or Half Court?

FOR MORE THAN 30 years, if we had only six or seven players, we played half court, but if we had eight or more, we played full. In December 2012, Danny McCoy, who started playing in the game in 1986, concluded that playing full-court was becoming too hard on his body. He proposed that we designate one day a week to play half court, thinking that he would play on that day but not on the other two days. He submitted a written proposal to the Commissioner, and the Commissioner flew it by the geezerhood. In my email to them, I wrote that "Given the number of knee braces worn on any given day, not to mention the number of geezers who are battling one aging or injury related issue or another, I think this proposal has merit." The geezers either agreed, or, at least, they did not disagree vehemently. The two physicians in the game, both high energy, and both a good bit younger than the average geezer, were resistant; one of them wrote, "I am officially not for it but understand why there would be interest in it." We did not have unanimous support. If we had really been running a Quaker meeting, and I was the Clerk, I would have asked these two if they were willing to "stand aside," which means that they would be willing to allow the decision to go forth but that they wished for their disagreement to be recorded. It was not a Quaker meeting, it was participatory autocracy, so I simply made the decision. Thus began a period known as "Half Court Mondays." For the next year or two, we always played half court on Monday, no matter how many players showed up, but on Wednesdays and Fridays, if we had eight or more players, we played full-court. One of the geezers even arranged for t-shirts that said "Half Court Monday: Half a Workout Since 2012."

One day while I had rotated out of a full-court game, I observed a few of the younger players racing up and down the court while the others watched, and I also observed lots of wild passes thrown out of bounds on aborted fast breaks. I could see that the full-court game had become ragged, and based on these observations, and comments from some geezers, I concluded that for most of us the full-court game was less fun than the half-court game. Either I suggested, or others did, that we just play half court all the time. Except for a few of the younger guys, there was general agreement. We have not played full-court in six or seven years.

A Foul or a Charge? Out on Me or Out on You?
Did that Ball Hit the Line? Walking?
The Strategic Use of Jump Balls.

KEEPING ARGUMENTS TO a minimum is one of our guiding principles. As anyone who has played pickup basketball, or anyone who has watched high school, college or pro basketball, knows, when an offensive player and a defensive player collide, they, their teammates, and the fans are not likely to agree on whether it was a foul or a charge. In pickup games, although there sometimes are long and heated discussions about this, rarely if ever is either player persuaded that the other is right. In college and the NBA these days, there are long stretches while the referees review tapes to try to determine just what happened. To avoid such discussions, and the ill-will they inevitably cause, and to keep the game moving, we have put a simple procedure in place: if there is a disagreement (about a charge, or about whether a ball hit the out of bounds line, or anything else) we try to keep the discussion to a minimum— we simply call it a jump ball, we rotate possession, and we keep playing.

Similarly, to keep arguments to a minimum, we encourage everyone to "respect the call" (at one point we also had a set of geezer t-shirts with "Respect the call" on the back). In some pickup games, only the person on offense can make a call. We encourage either player to make a call. That is, if you foul me, I can call it, but so, too, can I call it if I foul you (not only "can I," I should). There is no penalty for fouls (we don't take the time to shoot foul shots, as they apparently do, or once did, in a pickup game at the Winston-Salem YMCA), so there is no real deterrent to fouling someone, and some take advantage of this. I have at times sent emails to certain players encouraging them to foul people less frequently (and in some cases, less aggressively). These have been received with differing responses. One guy who received such an email (what the Quakers would call an "eldering" email) wanted to argue that we should then be more open to offensive fouls, because, he claimed, on some of the fouls that had been called against him he actually had been fouled. Another recipient of one of my eldering emails was offended enough that he disappeared for two years. Mostly, however, people try not to foul too much, or, if they do, they are given sufficient grief by those on the court to deter them from continuing to do so.

4 "Check Your Testosterone at the Door"

WE DO HAVE arguments now and then. People yell at each other, and, in some cases, walk off the court—sometimes to avoid saying something they regret or to prevent their anger from escalating to a physical confrontation.

In two incidents that took place a few years apart, when they reached a certain level of anger, two different geezers yelled "Suck my dick" at the person who angered them (it was the same person—no surprise there, as he has angered many people). I find it interesting that when they got this angry these ostensibly macho guys chose such a homoerotic phrase. Such outbursts, however, are rare.

We have had only three physical confrontations in our 44 years. The first happened long ago, either in 1981 or 1982. My memory of it is hazy, though I know it took place upstairs in the Crackerbox, and the perpetrator was a visiting professor in Economics on a two-year appointment whose game was more aggressive than we were used to. Something set him off, or, as is often the case, an accumulation of things set him off, and he went after the guy who was covering him. It didn't last long, we admonished him, and soon he was no longer at Guilford, so we did not have to deal with him, nor did we have to deal with actual fighting for about thirty years.

Then, in May 2011, we had another incident. It took place on a day when we had enough players for two games, and I was in the game on the other court. Suddenly I heard commotion from the other game, and I saw a bunch of guys gathered around two of our younger, more athletic players, who were tangled up on the floor, clearly in the midst of a fight. People pulled them apart, and I told them both to leave. One in particular wanted to explain to me what had happened, for he was quite sure that he was not at fault (as Bruce Springsteen says to a judge in the long introduction to one of his songs, "Guilty with an explanation"), but I was not interested in holding a trial at that time on the court. I told him I'd do some thinking and be in touch.

They left. We finished the games. I got a lot of advice in the locker room, some serious, some not, and in fact did spend a few hours thinking about what the most appropriate response might be. I then sent the following email to all the geezers:

Geezers,

I sent the tapes to David Stern, and he got back to me immediately.

No suspensions, but a warning to everyone. We not only need to respect the call, but in general we need to have less needling, less yapping, less trash talking, and less arguing. I know that all of these things are part of the give and take of pickup basketball, but they also can contribute to the accumulation of antagonism. I have no doubt that the altercation that took place today had its origins in games that have been played over the last few weeks or months, and was not caused simply by whatever took place on court #1.

Those of you who still are young enough to have a lot of testosterone need to check some of it at the door.

If you find yourself getting especially frustrated or angry, just call it a day and leave the game rather than letting your frustration or anger escalate. Over the years we have had very very few conflicts that have led to actual physical confrontations... but periodically various players have been frustrated or angry enough to leave early (including your commish, once—yes, it was Wineburg). In other basketball settings it might make sense to stand your ground (for example, if your coach is named Krzyzewski), but given the spirit of the geezer game it is better for you and for the long-term health of the game to call it a day.

So, no suspensions, but everyone is on probation.

RICHIE

*****A commissioner's work is never done*****

This email seemed to stem the tide. [1] But then, just about two years later, in April 2013, we had another confrontation, two different guys, not really a fight—one took a swing at another, and connected.

The two involved in this altercation had both played football in high school. The aggressor, who was about 5'11" and 200 pounds, was covering a bigger man, about 6'2" and 240. Apparently things were getting increasingly heated between them, which I had not noticed. If I had, I might have made a defensive shift so they wouldn't have continued to cover each

---

1. Both are still in the game.

other. I am not sure how long it took for things to escalate to the point of no return, but we were all stunned when a fist was thrown and contact was made, though I think the fist made contact with the recipient's shoulder, not his face. If, as I believe, Bruce Hornsby is correct when he sings in his classic song about pickup basketball, "Take Me to the old Playground," that "how you play is who you are," then it can be said with confidence that the guy who took the swing, now a former geezer, is prone to impulsivity, and is likely to act without a great deal of premeditation.

I told the guy who threw the punch to leave, and that I'd be in touch. He did, though after we finished playing, he came into the locker room to apologize. I said that we couldn't have fights in the geezer game, and that I'd let him know what the penalty would be. That afternoon, I wrote him an email telling him that he was suspended for a week. Here is the email I sent to him:

xxxxx,

We've been playing midday basketball here at Guilford for 37 years now, and we've had our share of conflict, arguments, hurt feelings, and people walking off the court angry. Including the confrontation that took place earlier today, we have had very few actual physical confrontations. The previous confrontation took place in May 2011. I am concerned about the quality of the game, and I am concerned about the safety of the (old and getting older) geezers who play, and therefore I don't think we can take today's event lightly. My initial thought was to suspend you for two weeks, but because you were thoughtful and contrite enough to come into the locker room and apologize, I am going to reduce it to one week.

Therefore, I'm asking you to take a week off, and rejoin the game whenever you are ready after next Wednesday, April 10.

I have cut and pasted below the email message I sent out on May 11, 2011, after the last incident. You, along with everyone else, received it, so you can assume that you, and everyone else, had been warned.

See you in a week.

RICHIE

This may have prevented another fight, but four months later I was still concerned about the physical play on the part of these two. I therefore sent one of those "eldering" emails I mentioned in the previous chapter to both the guy who threw the punch and the guy who received it. Here is what I wrote:

I'd also like to ask the two of you to try to cut back on squabbling and arguing, and to be careful about how physically you play. I've had various complaints from more than one geezer, and my own observation is that the frequency and level of disputes increases when either of you is in the game. I, of course, want to keep the game as friendly as possible, and as injury-free as possible. Thanks for keeping this in mind.

RICHIE

I shared this email with a few of the geezers. One responded in the following way: "AND that is why you are the Commissioner... nicely put... For 30 years I have waited for your book on bb demeanor and your demeanor in life... parallels and differences." Now, six or seven years later, the book you are reading is a belated effort to respond (in part) to his request.

There was a fourth physical confrontation, but I was not there and thus this is second-hand. In the mid- to late-1990s, before the Spears YMCA was built, there was a Y guy who played so aggressively that one of the geezers began to refer to him as Biff. One day, Biff threw an elbow at one of our bigger and stronger players, who then took a swing at Biff (and connected). The two of them apparently worked it out that day. However, Biff continued to play so aggressively that two geezers complained to the person who was running the facility, and he applied the standard penalty used by the YMCA—Biff was suspended for a month.

We have had no fights since 2013.

5   Off the Court

THERE IS SOME banter on the court during games (though not a lot of trash talking), some brief conversations before and between games, and actual discussions about injuries, vacations, restaurants, books, or any number of other topics in the locker room before and after we play. Basketball is a social game both on and off the court, and this banter, these conversations, and sometimes real discussions have very much contributed to the sense of community and to the game's longevity.

Some geezer dialogue takes place online. Periodically, I send emails to all of the geezers, reminding them when their annual (or semi-annual) payments are due, that the gym will be closed for certain holidays, or that we will not have a court because of summer camps, resurfacing the floors, or whatever. Sometimes I send injury reports—when someone gets hurt, the others want to know how that person is doing. Over the years, many players have sustained injuries, usually minor, but sometimes requiring them to see a doctor, a dentist, or to go to a hospital. Once, memorably, when a guy came down with a rebound and his knee gave out (bringing back memories to some of us of a long-ago injury to NFL quarterback Joe Theismann), he was carried off the court on a stretcher, definitely a career-ending injury. Most of the emails that I send generate few or no responses, but some have led to spirited exchanges.

The "Black Friday" emails

CONSIDER THE FOLLOWING chain of 16 emails, elicited by what I thought was a routine injury report, but which led to many responses over a four-day period, some humorous, some serious, about my use of the word "black" in the email's title.

1 *My email labeled "Black Friday," Nov. 6, 2004*

Geezers,

Friday took its toll. Though it looked like Bob Williams only pulled a muscle or some such, he actually broke a bone in his left foot. Details still to be determined, but he's in a cast, on crutches, and, though not in great pain, trying to figure out the ramifications (e.g., his car is stick shift). Andy was last seen with ice on his ankle.

For me, it seemed like the week went on forever. Sorry it ended with two injuries.

RICHIE

2 *First responder, Odell, Nov. 8 2004*

Why was Friday "black".....is "black" an adjective for "bad"????????

I love the geezer game........WHITE..... ODELL

3 *Next, Frank, Nov. 8, 2004*

Amen my black brother. I suggest to the commish that since he integrated geezer nation he has the responsibility of diversity and sensitivity training. He is to be commended for integrating above the population norm. I suggest that you, me, and Cook wear all white Wednesday with red, black, and green wrist-bands.

4   *Then, me again, Nov. 9, 2004*

Geezers,

I stand corrected by the Reverend Brother Odell, and I think Brother Frank's idea is a good one. I suggest we begin by addressing the following question, which I've been pondering:

Barack Obama, the Senator-elect from Illinois, is the son of an African father and a white mother. He was raised for a number of years in Hawaii by his white grandparents, and he attended the island's most elite private school, Punahou. Is he black? Why or why not?

Perhaps we can discuss this at the foul line, while people are shooting foul shots (oh, wait a minute, we don't shoot foul shots).

RICHIE

5   *Odell, Nov. 9, 2004*

GUYS...LET IT GO...........LET'S PLAY GEEZER BASKETBALL............BY THE WAY CHARLIE... WHAT COLOR IS THE BASKETBALL???????

6   *Rob, Nov. 9, 2004*

And in the immortal words of Freud, who spent countless hours pondering the implications of things, "sometimes a cigar is just a cigar."

7 *Odell, Nov. 9, 2010*

Rob, wasn't Freud....... "so smart that he lost his mind"...... "PSYCHO" or "PSYCHOPATHIC = engaging in amoral or antisocial acts without feeling remorse." Are you sure "sometimes a cigar is just a cigar", or a "BIG JOINT"...I MEAN THE GOOD STUFF...WITH A LITTLE "ANGELDUST" AS THE KICKER?????? REMEMBER....IT'S A REASON WHY THEY NAMED IT "ANGEL" DUST — — — —

8 *Frank, Nov. 9, 2004*

Look guys, I guess sarcasm does not come across well on a computer. Some of the responses show you get it, some do not. I respect each and every one of you. I am immensely thankful that you have allowed me the opportunity to be part of your group. So let us get over BLACK FRIDAY with no hard feelings and no hard fouls. I look forward to seeing you all tomorrow. Odell, I am still wearing WHITE and I want to be on the WHITE team.

9 *Odell, Nov. 9, 2004*

Dr.   Hatchett........IT'S   A   GOOD   THING THAT   I   WILL   BE   IN   RALEIGH,   NC   ON WEDNESDAY.........MAYBE   YOU   WILL   WIN   A GAME OR TWO, MAYBE THREE......I ALSO AGREE MY FRIEND THAT ENOUGH IS ENOUGH...AND I ALSO WANT TO BE ON THE WHITE TEAM...YOU CAN'T BLAME ME....WHEN I LOOKED AT MR. WEBSTER'S DEFINITION OF (black and white).

BLACK="(a)HARMFUL, EVIL, OR WICKED: A
BLACK HEART (b)indicating censure, disgrace, etc.: a
black mark on one's record (c)the color opposite to white."
WHITE= (a) AUSPICIOUS; FORTUNATE,
MORALLY PURE; INNOCENT. (b) Lacking malice;
harmless (c) the color opposite to black."
Wow .... ODELL

10 *Danny, Nov. 9, 2004*

Guys - thanks for the entertainment - I am at a Hilton in
Chicago and it is boring!

I am going to miss Frank in white but I will wear gray
on polka dot Friday! I actually like and RESPECT the
geezers that wear black every day (I can only imagine
how they describe the geezer game to others). I am only
about 50/50 on the guys that wear white!

11 *Bob, Nov. 9, 2004*

Guys,

I am continually amazed by how pervasive racism is in
our culture. Embedded in our language, most of our
institutions, etc.

While our game is mostly about exercise, play and
recreation, we do play on an educational institution.

Odell, thanks for raising the issue and making each of
us more aware.

BOB

p.s. Getting back to basketball is easier for some than
others of us.

12 *Claire, Nov. 9, 2004*

First, greetings to all from DC.

Second, to those who were injured on the sad Friday, I hope you heal well and quickly. Unfortunately, I know broken bones do not get hurried, so Bob Williams, I guess you will be out for a while. Sorry!

Third, the discussion has been interesting to read from this distance. Bob Williams, as we at Guilford say, "speaks my mind". Enjoy the basketball—no injuries, and cheers for pointing things out and kicking them around (maybe I should say passing them around).

CLAIRE

13 *Richard, Nov. 9, 2004*

Guys.... errr... Folks (don't forget sexism)...

14 *Lyn, Nov. 10, 2004*

Odell,

I have mixed emotions about the Commish's comments about "black" Friday.

Being half-Black[1], I am outraged on one hand—and ashamed on the other, by such a callous comment.

Always one to make peace, I will play for either team today—white or black. However, I only want to play on the offense.

LYN

---

1. Lyn revealed the next time he played that his mother's maiden name was Black.

15 Ron, Nov. 10, 2004

I have yet to comment on the current discussions running across the internet but I have found it fascinating and good fodder for the book I am writing.

The book is tentatively titled "Bald Like Me." Little has anyone known that I have disguised myself as a tall yet aging ball player who is follicly challenged with at least one bad knee, all to fit in with group of other aging men with varying degrees of hairlines, who feel a deep need to, dare I say,...sweat. In reality, I am 5'3" with a full head of hair, a graying beard, and a deadly 2-handed jump shot. Please keep it up. I have much yet to write and I have only gotten through the dedication to Wineburg part.

16 Craig, Nov. 10, 2004: "Enough Black v. White!"

I hate to have to come off the temporary D.L. to enter into this argument, but you all have left me no choice. I don't see the world in black or white. I don't see it as male or female. Those groups have been battling for years about who is and who isn't discriminating or being discriminated against. As far as I am concerned, the only group of people who have a right to complain about the way they have been portrayed are.... West Virginians. Yes, that's right. For years they have put up with being stereotyped as corn-cob pipe smoking, illiterate hillbillies.

Why, only this morning I heard on the radio "Why was the toothbrush invented in West Virginia?" The answer: "Because if it was invented in any other state, they would have called it a teethbrush." Now THAT'S WHAT I'M TALKIN ABOUT. People definitely should not repeat jokes like that.

Social Capital

WHEN PEOPLE PLAY ball together three times a week, for years and years, it is not surprising that when life's various necessities arise, they sometimes turn to their teammates, at times for services, and at times for recommendations or advice. A mortgage? A foot doctor? Who's a good cardiologist, or who should I see to check out my ailing knee?

What we generally think of as "networking," French sociologist Pierre Bourdieu called "social capital." By this fancy term he meant the benefits that can accrue from such contacts, and he wanted to contrast it with economic capital (money itself) and cultural capital (knowledge and skills). Bourdieu and many other sociologists have shown that those from the privileged classes not only have more economic capital, and more cultural capital, but they also have more social capital than those from the lower classes. If Bourdieu were analyzing our game (hard to imagine), he would not fail to notice that most of the players are well-educated professionals—we have some doctors, professors, engineers, and owners of local businesses (in a few cases, owners or presidents of businesses that employ hundreds of people and do business regionally or nationally). Bourdieu might or might not notice, but I have, that we have had no lawyers in the game—this, I have said only half-jokingly, might have contributed to our longevity.[2]

Bourdieu would observe that if I (a professor) want to redo my mortgage, or need a recommendation for a doctor who is really good (sports injury? prostate? you name it), one of my hoop buddies is likely to be helpful, or have contacts who might be helpful. By playing in the game, I have accrued

2. Technically we have had two lawyers play, one as a guest and another as a short-term participant until he accepted an out-of-town job. Neither achieved geezer status.

social capital. Not surprisingly, therefore, over the years, many geezers have made visits to the foot doctor who plays in the game (and consulted with him in the locker room), a number have arranged for mortgages and remortgages by the mortgage banker in the game, some have asked for, and gotten, recommendations about long-term life insurance from one of the players who owned an insurance agency, and some have asked for, and received, editorial help as they have worked on articles or books (including me, on this book). One of our many unwritten rules is that such consultations should take place in the locker room, but not on the court, especially during games.

Our game is not unusual in this respect. All groups are likely to provide the opportunity for participants to accrue social capital. The urologist I go to tells me that he took up hockey at the age of 35, that he now plays one night a week with a bunch of guys he otherwise would never have met, and that half of the men on his team are now his patients.

Over the years, therefore, the geezers have come to know one another on the court, but also off the court. They do business with each other, seek advice from one another, and some socialize. Some play golf together on non-basketball days.

People Die

SOME OF THOSE who have played in the geezer game have died, though thankfully not on the court. So, too, have geezers lost family members—numerous parents, a wife, and in one case, a daughter. The geezers have stepped up when these deaths have occurred. When the daughter of one of our players died in 2013, we quickly raised $300 to contribute to the organization designated in the obituary (the Gateway Education Center). When the wife of one of the geezers died in in 2017, a crew of 8-10 of the geezers drove to nearby Kernersville, NC, to attend the funeral. These off-court gestures have meant a lot to those dealing with death.

The Geezers Go to the Ballpark

WE ALSO HAVE had many social gatherings. For example, the geezers have gone, en masse, to watch Guilford's men's and women's basketball teams play, to watch the daughters of one of the guys play in a high school basketball tournament, and to a batting cage to settle a bet over whether one of the geezers, Bob Wineburg, a former college baseball player, could still, at the age of 64, hit a baseball coming at him at 90 miles per hour (he could). These excursions typically were followed by those in attendance going somewhere to drink beer.

One memorable occasion took us to the local minor league ballpark to see the Class A Greensboro Grasshoppers. In 2007, Danny McCoy, who at the time was working for MetLife, invited all the geezers to attend a game at the new ballpark. MetLife had a "luxury box" in the second deck above the first base line where one could sit on comfortable furniture, watch the game, and be served beer and sandwiches. Danny not only reserved the box for the geezers, but he arranged with the ballpark's powers that be for me (as Commissioner of the geezer game) to throw out the first pitch. That morning, I practiced in the street in front of my house with Bob Wineburg, my next-door neighbor. After trying many options, I decided to go with a Luis (Look Back at the Center Field Wall) Tiant delivery, and to throw a curve ball. I was one of three people throwing out "first pitches." The other two were six years old and ten years old (I was 62). Mine was the only one of the three pitches that made it to the plate without bouncing, though it was low and outside. When I made it up to the luxury box to join the other geezers, Frank Hatchett (an all-state guard when he played for the Greensboro Day School) raised his fist and said "Luis Tiant!"

Big-Number Birthdays

WE ALSO HAVE celebrated various big-number birthdays (those divisible by 5, or 10, or 25) by reserving a room at a restaurant or bar and meeting for beer, sometimes for dinner as well as beer. These have been spirited events, especially when Andy Casper, one of the (younger) geezers who grew up not only playing football, baseball, and basketball, but also the accordion, brought his instrument with him and part of the "program" consisted of him leading us in song (the highlight, a spirited rendition of "Country Roads," dedicated to Danny McCoy, a native of West Virginia—and proud of it). At some of these events, I have used a PowerPoint Presentation to give joke awards.

When I turned 70, in 2015, the geezers insisted that we go out for beer to celebrate my hitting such a momentous non-prime number. Reluctantly, I agreed, assuming that maybe someone would take over my role and be the emcee, giving me and others grief, with the kinds of fake awards that I often included. When Lisa and I got there, I was surprised to see a much bigger crew than usually attended these events, including many long-retired geezers who had not played in the game for years, even decades. When the program began, various guys spoke about the game, and my leadership, in very nice ways (it was not in any sense a roast). And then, much to my surprise, one of them announced that they had arranged to name one of the courts in Ragan-Brown after me and showed me a mock-up of what the court would look like. A sub-group of geezers had approached administrators at the college about this (including Jon, the VP), were told it could actually happen if some amount of money was raised. It was only when writing this account, four years after the event, that it occurred to me to ask how much it took. Apparently in an exploratory meeting at the Mexican restaurant across the street from the college, each of five or six geezers on the "planning team" was challenged by Jon to put up $500 toward the needed fund-raising goal, which was not specified. They all agreed to pony up that amount (how about that!) and then some effort was made to raise additional money from other geezers. My guess is that between $3,000 and $10,000 was raised (and my wife tells me that she heard that the actual amount was $7,000).

Just as he had arranged for the clock and the plaque that the geezers had purchased to be mounted on the wall a few years earlier, Jon arranged for my name to be applied to the court, just like Mike Krzyzewski's at Duke.[3] A few weeks later, there it was (it says, "Richie's Court: Richie 'The Commish' Zweigenhaft").

As also noted above, Jon lost his job a month or so later, without warning, escorted off campus with his personal effects—gone but not forgotten, neither seen nor heard from since. The geezers had mixed feelings, depending in part on whether they had to cover, or be covered by, him. There was, however, consensus on one thing: as one geezer put it, "Glad we got Richie's name on the court before Jon's departure."

In June 2016, Steve Schlehuser, the oldest guy in the game, celebrated his 75th birthday. We generally referred to him as "Old Steve" until he turned 65 in 2006, at which point, as a sign of respect, we began to call him "Steve the Elder." Five years later, when he turned 70, we began to call him "Steve the Really Elder." At a celebration we had for his 75th birthday, I suggested that we should call him "Steve the Really, Really Elder," and that when he got to be 80 we should call him "Steve

3. I have joked many times that this is the only thing Coach K and I have in common.

the Ancient." For that 75th birthday celebration, we rented a back room at a restaurant, invited wives and partners, drank beer, listened to and sang along with music on the accordion by Andy Casper, and had a PowerPoint-guided "program," complete with awards (e.g., Rookie of the Year, shared by Todd Clark and Tim Murphy, Most Improved Player, won by Mark Harris, Best Comeback from Surgery, shared by Andy Casper and Rob Luisana, Most Banked in Threes, won—no contest— by Thom Espinola, and the Stephen Curry Award, won by Frank Hatchett). A good time was had by all.

Trump

A FEW MONTHS later, Trump was elected. We have not had a celebratory all-geezer gathering, birthday or otherwise, since that election. I have a very clear memory of eating lunch with a few geezers one Friday (a subgroup of us often have lunch together after the games on Friday). It was March 2016, a week or so before the North Carolina primary, and we were eating at a Mexican restaurant across the street from the college. One of the guys who was there (an outspoken liberal) asked another (an outspoken conservative) if he was going to vote for Trump. The conservative said that Trump was not his first choice, "but," he went on to say, "I can live with Trump."

I grew up in a Jewish family, and my undergraduate honors thesis was a psychological analysis of Hitler's personality. In doing the research for the thesis, in discussions with my thesis advisor (an eminent Russian historian, also Jewish), and in the years since, I have read about, and thought about, how Hitler had enough popular support to become Chancellor of Germany in 1933. Sitting there in the Mexican restaurant, I had a very eerie feeling. I could not shake this image that we were sitting in a restaurant in Germany in January 1933 (probably not a Mexican restaurant), and this friendly, educated, and good-natured guy that I play basketball with (in Germany in 1933 we more likely would have been playing soccer), might have said, casually, that Hitler wasn't his first choice, but he could live with him.

Trump won the North Carolina primary, edging out Ted Cruz, 40% to 37%. As the 2016 election approached, and Trump had become the Republican nominee, it was clear that some of those in the geezer game were going to vote for him, and a few were outspoken Trump supporters. Two of the geezers, memorably (to me), made clear that they thought that both Donald Trump and Hillary Clinton were awful and that it wouldn't matter which was elected. At least one geezer proudly informed the others of us that he had been driving Trump voters to the polls for early voting and planned to do so on election day. When Trump was elected, I was devastated, and I knew that some of the Trump-supporting geezers were celebrating (they were, perhaps, every bit as happy as I had been when Obama was elected). The next day was Wednesday, a basketball day, but I had no classes, and no office hours, and no (real) committee meetings, so I stayed home. I did not want to see anyone, especially those who had happily voted for Trump.

For the most part, Trump's election has not affected the game. We still play three days a week, and I no longer think to myself, every time I see those who voted for Trump, "How could that guy have supported such a crude, narcissistic, misogynistic, racist, wanna-be dictator?" Nor have I asked any of them if they still support him, or if they will vote for him again in 2020. As I have indicated, one of my guiding principles when it comes to the geezer game is to try to minimize arguments. I will admit that if I were a more tolerant person perhaps I'd be willing, perhaps even eager, to talk about these profound differences in world-view over a beer with these guys, but I'm not. So far, at least, I have not been willing to resume my role as the social chairman who arranges geezer-inclusive celebrations for big birthdays. Maybe I will once again want to enjoy everyone's company in that way. Meanwhile, the game goes on, having survived differences among the players about Ronald Reagan, the two Bushes, Bill Clinton, and Barack Obama. Maybe the game (and the country) will survive Trump.

6 *Some Reasons for the Game's Longevity*

IT IS IMPOSSIBLE, of course, to know why the game has lasted as long as it has. Many factors have been at play, and I am sure it is the confluence of these, plus many I am not aware of, along with a dollop (or maybe more) of good luck. The ones that come to mind are the following:

1 Good guiding principles, accepted by those who play. Among these are the ones I listed at the end of the opening chapter: 1) everyone plays an equal amount; 2) injuries and arguments are to be minimized; and 3) friendship first.

2 What I have called "participatory autocracy," in which everyone's voice is heard but ultimately I have made a decision (without actual votes almost all of the time and without the need for consensus). This may not be as unQuakerly as it sounds. Even in a Quakeresque setting such as the college where I teach, there are times when consensus has not been reached but a decision must be made (deadlines, for example, require someone, often the

President, sometimes the Board, to make a choice to go one way or another).

3   Back in 2003, negotiating a good, long-term, working agreement with the college to rent a court three times a week. Here, again, the wise decision of Guilford's former President, Kent Chabotar, to allow the nonGuilfordians to continue to play in the Guilford gym, should be applauded.

4   The willingness to adjust, as is most apparent in the many rule changes we have enacted over time—especially adding the three-point shot, trying Half Court Mondays for a year or two, and the subsequent switch to half court all the time.

5   Keeping the game competitive but not allowing it to become too aggressive. Keeping it competitive has included efforts to make teams that are well-matched, so that the games will be close. Keeping it from getting too competitive has been a bigger challenge. As I have indicated, we have had a few physical confrontations but, fortunately, only a few.

6   Having a woman in the game. From the time we started playing back in 1976 in the Crackerbox, until she retired from teaching at Guilford in 2013, Claire Morse, my colleague in the psychology department, was a regular participant. At times, other women have played, but none as frequently or for as many years as Claire. When she and her husband lived in El Salvador in the early 1970s, she practiced with the women's national team. Although she was never a dominant player in our game, and typically was not a high scorer, she might have one of the highest "career" shooting percentages of anyone who has played. Moreover, and this is the point I want to make here, the fact that we usually had a woman on the court helped us establish values that have contributed to the game's longevity. That is to say, I believe our game has

been less aggressive than it might have been and has had less stereotypical macho behavior (fights? arguments? trash talking?) because on most days there was a female presence—and especially because it was Claire, who is consistently good-natured, fair, and cares about people's feelings.

7 Having a core of players who have been around for a long time. This includes academics with tenure (because of tenure, they were not going to lose their teaching jobs unless they committed what used to be called "moral turpitude") but also Greensboro residents who did not change jobs a lot, or, if they did change jobs, were still able to play basketball a few times a week in the middle of the day. Also: we have been fortunate to have doctors (especially when there were injuries) and, I suspect, fortunate not to have lawyers.

Perhaps these things contributed to the longevity of the game, and perhaps they can provide some guidance for others hoping to keep their pickup basketball games going. Who knows, maybe some of these factors, and some of the ideas I have shared in this quirky little account might help in non-basketball settings, as people try to keep other games going, or, in work settings, as they try to keep everyone involved and arguments and fights to a minimum. Friendship first. Respect the call. You don't stop playing because you grow old; you grow old because you stop playing.

Epilogue
The Return of the Geezer Game

IN THE FIRST EDITION of this book, I wrote: "Maybe the game (and the country) will survive Trump." After a 22-month hiatus because of the coronavirus, the game resumed on January 31, 2022. Whether the country survives Trump remains to be seen.

When the pandemic hit North Carolina, in mid-March 2020, just one month after *GEEZERBALL* was published, Guilford College, like most other schools in the state, closed all buildings. It was the middle of spring break, so the students were not on campus. An email from the college president informed students and faculty that spring break was to be extended for a week, and then all classes were to shift to an online format for two weeks. This shift to online classes ended up being for the rest of the semester, and for the entire 2020-2021 academic year. The gym, too, was closed, and so the geezer game was finished, at least for the time being. I did not touch a basketball for almost a year. Deprived of the three-times-a-week geezer game, I turned to riding my mountain bike, which turned out to be surprisingly therapeutic. I wrote an article about this for the local paper, titled "How cycling has become therapy for me at age 75."[1]

In that article, in addition to recounting various therapeutic benefits that biking had provided me during the pandemic, I found myself contemplating just how different these two forms of exercise are. Basketball is communal, whereas riding the bike (for me, at least, most of the time) is solitary. Moreover, unlike basketball, biking gives one a chance to think about all kinds of things. Away from the computer, away from the TV and other media, away from the phone (well, I keep one in my pocket but I almost never take it out of that pocket), when on my bike I find myself pondering the existential questions, planning future activities, reminding myself about things I need to do or people I want to contact, and sometimes composing passages that I subsequently use in articles or books that I am writing.

In contrast, in my many decades playing basketball, when on the court I rarely think about anything other than what is right in front of me: the ball, the guy I am covering, and whether any of my teammates are open for a pass. The (mostly) solitary nature of biking is a cognitive experience, quite different from the communal game of basketball. Whereas some of my favorite moments on the bike have involved thinking, many of my favorite moments on the basketball court have involved no thought at all, just instinctive reactions.

Much as I liked, and still like, biking, and much as I appreciate the many benefits it provided when we lost the geezer game, I really missed playing basketball.

Eight months into my almost-daily biking regime, the 2020 presidential election took place. Joe Biden soundly defeated

1. Zweigenhaft, Richie (2022). "How cycling has become therapy for me at age 75," *News & Record*, June 19, 2022; https://greensboro.com/opinion/columnists/richie-zweigenhaft-how-cycling-has-become-therapy-for-me-at-age-75/article_ab335460-ec19-11ec-8551-ffe21c4aae2d.html

Donald Trump (though, as we all know, Trump and many of his cult-like followers refused to acknowledge his defeat). Whereas in 2016 it was pretty clear to those of us in the game which geezers had supported Trump, by the November 2020 election we had not played for eight months, and therefore I have no idea if the 2016 Trump supporters voted for Trump again in the 2020 election (or, for that matter, if any of them went to Washington, D. C. on January 6, 2021, as part of the attempted coup; to my knowledge, none of the Trump-supporting geezers have been arrested for participating in the insurrection).

The first vaccines became available in North Carolina in early January 2021, and, because I was over 75, I was among the first to be vaccinated. I had the second of two shots by early February. By April, Brian Lampkin, a regular in the geezer game since 2015, a co-owner of Scuppernong books, and the editor of the book you hold in your hands, had also been vaccinated. Thirteen months after the last geezer game on campus, he and I arranged to meet on a Tuesday morning at an outdoor court to shoot baskets. We shot around for a while, and then decided to play one-on-one (we played cautiously, masked, and with minimal defense, kind of like the NBA all-star game). We enjoyed it so much that we did the same thing for the next two Tuesdays (by the second or third week we took the masks off). I then sent an email to all of the geezers and invited them—if and only if they had been vaccinated—to join us, warning them that the cement surface not only posed injury risks, but that it might be hard on their (aging) bodies. Two geezers showed up the next Tuesday (Charlie Johnson, age 73, having had surgery on both knees a few years ago, and Ron Irons, age 68, who also had had knee surgery, but only on one knee). We played two-on-two. It went well (fun, competitive, no injuries) and a few weeks later, two more geezers joined us (Tim Murphy, a baby at age 57, back from Hawaii where he and his wife live for part of each year, and Rob Luisana, age 72, who had hip surgery in 2019). We played either two-on-two or three-on-three for the next few months, depending on how many showed up. There were a few falls, with a bit of blood drawn here and there, but no real injuries, and we had fun.

Sometimes there were guys shooting at the other hoop, and in a few cases they asked to join our game. Before we let them play, I always asked if they had been vaccinated. Of the six or seven guys who asked to play over a period of a few months, all of whom were in their late teens or twenties, most had not been vaccinated, and I told them that they could not play with us. Usually I noted that our policy was the same as the one that the city of New York applied to the Brooklyn Nets' Kyrie Irving, who had refused to be vaccinated, and therefore was not allowed to play in their home games. Each time this happened, they were nice about it, and seemed to be understanding, though I doubt if it affected their intentions about getting vaccinated—they probably simply assumed that we were old, and were being cautious (or over-cautious), but I don't think they thought this had anything to do with them or their decision not to get vaccinated.

In one case, a 38-year-old told us that he had been vaccinated, and he not only played with us that day, but he returned four or five times to play in our Sunday game. By this time, we were playing on Tuesdays and Sundays, so he could not play on Tuesdays because he had work commitments during the week. A former AAU player whose skills were far beyond ours, he had an easy-going personality, he clearly liked playing with us, and we liked having him in the game. Having just moved here from Detroit, he was looking for a reasonably-proced place to rent for himself, his wife, and his daughter. As luck would have it, Tim's wife knew of a friend seeking to rent a house, and it worked out for everyone. So social capital continued to enter the dynamics of our little outdoor game, just as it had in the indoor game.

By June 2021, Guilford College was starting to open up a bit, with plans for in-person classes in the forthcoming fall semester. When I saw that the college was once again going to rent summer space to the Eastern Music Festival (EMF), as it had every summer since 1961 except for the summer of 2020, I wrote to Jim Hood, who had become the college's second interim president during the pandemic[2] to see if the geezers could return to the gym. I assured Jim that we would be willing to show that we had been vaccinated, that we would sign an insurance waiver, and that we would be glad to forego use of a locker room.

Jim was encouraging, and shared my email with Jermaine Harris, who was then the head of the COVID Task Force on campus. When three weeks went by without my hearing further, I wrote again to see what was up. Jim again responded quickly, and again encouragingly, and this time told me that Bill Foti, the new Athletic Director (Guilford's fifth athletic director in the last five years[3]), would be the person I'd need to work with. After a week went by, and I had not heard from him, I emailed him and explained who the geezers were, and what we were

2. For my version of how Jim was appointed Interim President, see the Epilogue to *Jews, Palestinians, and Friends* in Part One of this volume, starting on page 91.

3. Tom Palumbo has been the men's basketball coach since 2003. He was also the athletic director from 2007 until 2017. After he "stepped down" (not sure if that is the right term—there was a Title IX lawsuit, and who was doing what and why became quite murky) as athletic director, over the next four years there were four interim athletic directors, for varying lengths of time (Nelson Bobb, Craig Eilbacher, Sue Bower and Sharon Beverly). Bill Foti was hired in June 2021. Even with the merry-go-round of leadership in athletics at Guilford between 2017 and 2020, the geezer game had been mostly unaffected—until COVID.

seeking. He wrote back, promptly, and encouragingly, and told me that he was in the process of hiring a new director for the athletic facility and that once the new director and staffing were in place, and assuming the new Delta variant did not pose the need for new precautions that would keep the geezers from playing, someone would be in touch and we could then work out the details for the return of the geezer game.

The Delta variant, however, did call for renewed precautions, at Guilford and throughout the country. I did not hear again from Guilford about a return of the geezer game for another five months. In late November 2021, I sent another email to Bill Foti. By this time, the small group of us playing outside had moved our playing time both on Tuesdays and Sundays from 10 a.m. to 1 p.m. because we no longer needed to beat the heat— it was late fall, and in fact some days were quite chilly (that is putting it mildly—we played one day when it was 28 degrees). I explained to Bill Foti that those of us who were playing in this outdoor game were exploring indoor options, one of which was the downtown YMCA, where there is a cost for joining and a monthly fee. I reminded him that over the years we had paid about $4,000 a year to Guilford, and that I'd much prefer for our money to go to Guilford than the Y (though I like the Y a lot).

He responded immediately and indicated that he thought that we should be able to work something out. He passed my email on to Ryan Madison, who had been hired as Director of the P. E. Center, and Ryan soon contacted me. He was quite enthusiastic. He told me that once he knew the spring semester practice schedules for the men's and women's basketball teams, he would be back in touch.

Then, just as the Delta variant had bollixed up our plan to resume indoor play in August, the Omicron variant arrived. I didn't hear from Ryan for a month. The Omicron virus was spreading throughout the country, and Guilford, like many other schools, in early January was forced to cancel men's and women's basketball games because of cluster infections. Some colleges had announced that they were enforcing mandates for booster shots. Guilford did not do that initially, but in early January it did announce that students, staff, and faculty would have to get the booster shot by February 15. In addition, it shifted the first two weeks of classes from in-person to online.

Ryan scheduled a Zoom meeting late in January with me and Assistant Commissioner Danny McCoy to discuss the logistics for a return of the geezers to Ragan Brown. I had decided that we should start by playing twice a week, not our former three times a week, just to see how much interest there was. After all, the geezers were two years older, many were probably 10-20 pounds heavier, at least one had a serious bout with the first wave of COVID that required him to be hospitalized for six days (and then he got it again!), some had newly diagnosed health issues, and one had surgery for a blocked carotid artery. Our old patched up crew was likely to be even more decrepit than in the past, so starting with two days a week seemed to make more sense than three.

At that Zoom meeting we determined that the geezers could reserve the Richie Court Mondays and Fridays. Because the college required all students, faculty, and staff to have received vaccinations and booster shots, so too would we require the geezers to have done so. Similarly, because the college (and the county) at that time required wearing masks for all indoor group activities, we would require masks. We would have a locker room in which we could change—but no access to showers. When I sent an email to the twenty-two geezers then on the email list informing them of these ground rules and asking them to send me the dates that they had received vaccinations and booster shots, all but one sent me those dates, and many included messages indicating that they were eager to play again. The one exception was a geezer who wrote that he was "not planning to get a booster shot at this time." In my response to him, I made it clear that he could not rejoin the game without getting the booster shot and told him that if he decided to get the booster to let me know. About a month later, he sent me evidence that he had gotten the booster, and rejoined the game.[4]

The geezer game returned on January 31, 2022. Twelve geezers showed up. Eight played, four on four, our usual games to 30 (threes counting as three, all other baskets counting as two); the other four guys decided on this first day back just to shoot around at the other basket and then they sat on some nearby bleachers and kibitzed, schmoozed, and heckled. A good time was had by all. After a twenty-month hiatus, the game was back.

Now, as I write this (early September, 2022), we have been back for more than six months, playing twice a week on Mondays and Fridays. The attendance has been steady, averaging twelve on Mondays, ten on Fridays (the most we have had was 15, and twice we have had only six). We wore masks for the first seven weeks, but then the college announced that as a result of having tested all faculty, staff, and students, and the declining rates of infection in Guilford County, it was moving to what it called Phase 4 of its health and safety protocols, and masks were optional indoors on campus. The geezers immediately took off the masks. Then, in late June, because the number of those infected with COVID on campus had continued to go down, the college shifted from Phase 4 to Phase 5 of its health and safety protocols, and this

4. Some readers, and probably most of the geezers, will not be shocked to learn that this booster holdout was also the most vociferous Trump supporter in 2016.

meant that we again had access to a shower room. Recently, however, yet another variant, this one called BA.5, has been sweeping the nation.

A few geezers decided not to return to the game because of nagging injuries, or fear of recurring injuries. At least one indicated to me that he was worried about the game functioning as a superspreader of the virus. He was not only worried about the Trump supporters and their tendency to ignore the risks of the virus, but the people they spend time with. So far, only one geezer has reported having tested positive (after a trip abroad). He waited until he tested negative, waited another ten days before playing, played once (and played well)—and then had a kickback recurrence of COVID. None of the other nine geezers who played the day he played subsequently got it.

Although most days the games have been competitive and good natured, at times there have been minor disputes, and some days there is muttering or grumbling about calls, teammates, or opponents. There have been a few collisions, and once in a while some blood has been drawn, but, so far, no stitches (though one guy probably should have gotten stitches for a collision that had him bleeding from the mouth not only immediately afterwards but he was still bleeding, or started bleeding again, three days later, the next time we played). There was an injury in late November when Craig Chappelow broke a finger going for a loose ball (he had surgery a few days later). When he called to schedule an appointment with his doctor, the receptionist looked up his record and asked "Is this another basketball injury?"

One geezer reported to me, a few days after it happened, that when he got around his defender, this guy stuck out his leg to trip him, like the memorable series of fouls in 2016 by Duke's Grayson Allen in which Allen tripped opponents, first against Louisville, then against Florida State, and then, a few months later, against Elon. Allen was called for flagrant fouls in both the Louisville and Florida State games, and the day after the Florida State game he was "reprimanded" by the ACC.[5] After the Elon game, the third offense in a matter of months, Mike Krzyzewski, the Duke coach, bristled when asked about what many saw as very minimal consequences for Allen's transgressions: "I handle things the way I handle them. I think I've handled this correctly, and moving forward, I will continue to handle it correctly. I don't need to satisfy what other people think I should do. I'm a teacher and a coach, and I'm responsible for that kid. I know him better than anybody, and so to think that it's the last thing that's said about this to him is wrong."[6] Coach K gave Allen an "indefinite suspension," but kept him out for only one game.[7]

I did not see the offense at Guilford (like every basketball fan in America, I saw replays of Grayson Allen's), though right after it happened I did hear the usually mild-mannered geezer who was almost tripped call his defender out about something, I wasn't quite sure what at the time.[8] When he told me this story,

5. Hamilton, Brian, "After second trip, Duke needs Grayson Allen to keep his cool," Sports Illustrated, February 26, 2016; https://www.si.com/college/2016/02/27/duke-grayson-allen-tripping-incidents-acc

6. Laird, Sam, "Grayson Allen and the arrogant sanctimony of Duke's Coach K," *Mashable*, December 22, 2016; https://mashable.com/article/grayson-allen-duke-coach-k

7. Chase, Chris, "What a Joke! Coach K ends Grayson Allen's 'Indefinite Suspension' after just one game," Fox Sports, January 4, 2017; https://www.foxsports.com/stories/college-basketball/what-a-joke-coach-k-ends-grayson-allens-indefinite-suspension-after-just-one-game. Coach K is not one of my role models—see p. 174, note 3.

8. As was the case for my description of a few of the more embarrassing moments in Geezer history described in the first edition (see pp. 157–158), I have chosen to follow the path taken by the late great Warren Zevon (in his classic song, "Poor, Poor, Pitiful Me"): "I ain't namin' names."

however, my commissioner's antenna went up, and I realized that I had better watch this transgressor much more carefully.

In my presence, there has been no political talk. More specifically, even with the January 6 Committee airing its explosive (and to my mind riveting) hearings on national television, and the National Archives and the FBI finding more than 300 classified documents illegally and apparently casually stored at Mar-a-Lago, I have heard no mention of Trump. Therefore, I don't know (and don't really want to know) if I am again playing with people who continue to support the narcissist with a mafia-like leadership style, a man who moved the country dangerously close to autocratic rule and fascism, and who, if there is any accountability in our system, should end his life in jail.

For now, however, the geezer game goes on.

Appendices

Appendix 1.   Table on Jewish voting, 1916-2016.[1]

YEAR	CANDIDATE	PERCENT OF JEWISH VOTE	PERCENT OF NAT'L VOTE
1916	Hughes (R)	45	46
	Wilson (D)	55	49
1920	Harding (R)	43	60
	Cox (D)	19	34
	Debs (Socialist)	38	3
1924	Coolidge (R)	27	54
	Davis (D)	51	29
	LaFollette (P)	22	17
1928	Hoover (R)	28	58
	Smith (D)	72	41
1932	Hoover (R)	18	40
	Roosevelt (D)	82	57
1936	Landon (R)	15	37
	Roosevelt (D)	85	61
1940	Wilkie (R)	10	45
	Roosevelt (D)	90	55
1944	Dewey (R)	10	46
	Roosevelt (D)	90	53
1948	Dewey (R)	10	45
	Truman (D)	75	50
	Wallace (Progressive)	15	2
1952	Eisenhower (R)	36	55
	Stevenson (D)	64	44
1956	Eisenhower (R)	40	57
	Stevenson (D)	60	42
1960	Nixon (R)	18	50
	Kennedy (D)	82	50
1964	Goldwater (R)	10	38
	Johnson (D)	90	61

1. From   https://www.jewishvirtuallibrary.org/jewish-voting-record-in-u-s-presidential-elections

YEAR	CANDIDATE	PERCENT OF JEWISH VOTE	PERCENT OF NAT'L VOTE
1968	Nixon (R)	17	43
	Humphrey (D)	81	43
	Wallace (Independent)	2	13
1972	Nixon (R)	35	61
	McGovern (D)	65	38
1976	Ford (R)	27	48
	Carter (D)	71	50
1980	Reagan (R)	39	51
	Carter (D)	45	41
	Anderson (I)	15	6
1984	Reagan (R)	31	59
	Mondale (D)	57	41
1988	Bush (R)	35	53
	Dukakis (D)	64	46
1992	Bush (R)	11	37
	Clinton (D)	80	43
	Perot (Independent)	9	19
1996	Dole (R)	16	41
	Clinton (D)	78	49
	Perot (Independent)	3	8
2000	Bush (R)	19	48
	Gore (D)	79	48
	Nader (Independent)	1	2
2004	Bush (R)	24	51
	Kerry (D)	76	48
2008	McCain (R)	22	46
	Obama (D)	78	53
2012	Romney (R)	30	47
	Obama (D)	69	51
2016	Trump (R)	24	46
	Clinton (D)	71	48

Appendix 2.   Voices for Peace flyer, April 2005.

Sponsored by a wide variety of Guilford College organizations and funded by the Guilford Initiative on Faith & Practice, made possible by a grant from the Lilly Foundation.

Voices from Palestine and Israel:
"Living for Peace" in a Holy Land

During two days at Guilford College, six distinguished visitors will share their insights and expertise on diverse aspects of the Israel-Palestine conflict. They also will share the stories of their lives and their calling to "live for peace" between Israelis and Palestinians.

The Colloquium includes a major public session on April 7 at 7:30 p.m. in Dana Auditorium, smaller gatherings for members of the Guilford and Greensboro communities, seminars with assigned readings, and informal opportunities for students to explore how to discern a life vocation.

In recent years, Guilford College has sought ways to improve communication, and deepen relationships, among Israelis, Palestinians and Americans. Last summer Max Carter, director of Friends Center, Campus Ministry and Quaker Studies, his wife Jane Carter, and Rabbi Jonathan W. Malino, professor of philosophy and John A. Weissenfluh professor of ethics and religion, co-led a three-week work-study trip to Israel and Palestine, sponsored by Friends United Meeting. The Guilford Colloquium will recreate, for a larger audience, some of the enlightening and inspiring moments of that trip.

Funded by a grant from the Lilly Foundation, Voices from Palestine and Israel: "Living for Peace" in a Holy Land" is

April 6, 2005

8:15 - 10 p.m. General Presentation 1: **Joseph M. Bryan Jr. Auditorium** *open to the public.*
Voices from Palestine and Israel: Personal, Vocational and Family Life in a Contested Land

April 7, 2005

Noon-1 p.m. Lunch Meetings *assigned reading:*
(1) **Discussion with Yehuda Gellman: Jewish Text Study on the "Binding of Isaac"**
(Dining Hall Small Walnut Room)
(2) **Discussion with Raja Zeedani: Managing Hotel Housekeeping in a Divided City: Stories from the Front Lines** (Dining Hall Large Walnut Room)
(3) **Discussion with Edna Ullmann-Margalit: Philosophy of Science Meets Holy Land History and Archaeology** (Frank Science Building Library)

2:10 - 4 p.m. General Presentation 2: **Joseph M. Bryan Jr. Auditorium** *open to the public.*
Voices from Palestine and Israel: Prospects for Peace between Israelis and Palestinians.

7:30 - 9:30 p.m. General Presentation 3: **Dana Auditorium** *open to the public.*
Voices from Palestine and Israel: Challenges to "Living for Peace" in a Holy Land.

April 8, 2005

8:30 - 9:45 a.m. Breakfast Meetings *assigned reading.*
(1) **Book Discussion: Buruma and Margalit, Occidentalism**
(Frank Science Building Library)
(2) **Discussion: How the Israeli and Palestinian Media Cover the Israel/Palestine Conflict**
(Alumni House)

Avishai Margalit, professor of philosophy at the Hebrew University and currently a visiting professor at New York University, is one of Israel's most distinguished philosophers, activists (Peace Now, B'Tselem), and political thinkers. Avishai writes regularly about the Israeli-Palestinian conflict for the *New York Review of Books*, and is the author of *Idolatry* (with Moshe Halbertal), *The Decent Society*, *Occidentalism* (with Ian Buruma) and *The Ethics of Memory*.

Raja Zeedani, trained in social work and linguistics, worked as chief translator for the Palestine Press Services. From 1988–2001 she held a variety of management positions, including manager of housekeeping at the Hyatt Hotel in Jerusalem. In 1999 the Hyatt Hotel recognized her with a Special Achievement Award. Currently Raja is a producer with the Middle East Broadcasting Company.

Yehuda Gellman, professor of philosophy at Ben Gurion University of the Negev and senior fellow at the Shalom Hartman Institute for Judaic Studies in Jerusalem, is author of numerous articles and books on religious experience, the biblical story of the binding of Isaac from Jewish and Christian perspectives, mysticism, and Judaism and feminism. A religiously observant Jew, he is father of eight children. His sons have combined service in the Israeli Army with traditional yeshiva study. Yehuda has been active in interfaith meetings in Israel, Rome and the United States and is a member of the Association for Civil Rights in Israel.

Sari Nusseibeh, president of al-Quds University in Jerusalem and professor of philosophy, is the co-author, with former Israeli security chief, Ami Ayalon, of the Nusseibeh-Ayalon Plan. In conjunction with the plan, Sari is leading the People's Campaign for Peace and Democracy to gain support for a two-state solution to the Israeli-Palestinian Conflict. In 2002 Sari was profiled in the *New Yorker*, and last summer his People's Campaign was featured in the *Jerusalem Report* under the title "Palestinian Peace Now." Sari is a fellow at the Radcliffe Institute of Harvard University.

Edna Ullmann-Margalit, professor of philosophy and education at the Hebrew University and currently a fellow at the Russell Sage Foundation in New York, has written books on ethics, philosophy of science and the Dead Sea Scrolls, and has translated Ludwig Wittgenstein's *Philosophical Investigations* from German into Hebrew. Edna is former chair of the Association for Civil Rights in Israel, and former vice president of the New Israel Fund, a major American philanthropic organization that supports Israeli and Palestinian programs devoted to democracy, human rights and equality.

Said Zeedani, assistant to the president of al-Quds University for Community Relations and professor of philosophy, has written extensively on liberal democracy and human rights, the Israeli-Palestinian conflict and issues related to the nearly 20% of Israeli citizens who are Palestinians. He recently completed four years as director of the Palestinian Independent Commission for Citizens' Rights, the national human rights commission of Palestine, founded to advance human rights under the Palestinian Authority.

Driving to Guilford College? Daytime parking will be available near the Frank Family Science Building. Wednesday night, parking will be available at New Garden Friends Meeting. Thursday night, parking will be behind Dana Auditorium and at New Garden Friends Meeting. For more information, contact Jonathan W. Malino, tel. 336-316-2223; JMalino@guilford.edu.

Appendix 3.   AAUP flyer, November 2020.

Guilford College Faculty Targeted for Termination

selected accomplishments and awards

DAMON AKINS (2007)
Associate Professor of History

Co-author of *We Are the Land: A History of Native California*, with William J. Bauer, Jr. (University of California Press, 2021)

DAVE LIMBURG (1993)
Professor of Modern Language Studies

Recipient of the Bruce B. Stewart Teaching Award, Dick Dyer Awards, and a CPPS fellowship; leader of numerous study-abroad programs to Germany

PHILIP SLABY (2005)
Associate Professor of History

Author of multiple scholarly articles, book reviews, and national/international conference papers; peer reviewer for the *Journal Enterprise & Society*

MARIA BOBROFF (2004)
Professor of Modern Language Studies

Author of multiple peer-reviewed chapters, articles, and national/international conference papers; recipient of seven grants from the French-American Cultural Exchange Foundation

CHRISTIAN MATHES (2018)
Visiting Assistant Professor of Justice and Policy Studies

Author of multiple scholarly articles, book chapters and conference papers; co-editor of *Migration Policy and Practice: Interventions and Solutions* (Palgrave, 2016)

JANET STARMER (2006)
Visiting Instructor of Modern Languages and Language Lab Supervisor

14 years of teaching and service at Guilford

FRANK BOYD (2017)
Provost and Professor of Political Science

Three years of administration, teaching, and service at Guilford

MARLENE McCAULEY (1986)
Charles A. Dana Professor of Geology and Sustainable Food Systems

34 years of teaching, service, and administration at Guilford

CHARLIE TEFFT (1999)
Half-Time Instructor of Art

Guilford College alum; studio artist; 21 years of teaching and service at Guilford

SARAH THOELEN (2017)

Assistant Professor of History

Author of *Greater Than Equal: African American Struggles for Schools and Citizenship in North Carolina, 1919-1965* (University of North Carolina Press, 2013)

LISA McLEOD (1999)

Professor of Philosophy

Recipient of the DuBois Award and the Dick Dyer Award; author of multiple scholarly articles/chapters and conference papers

DAVE DOBSON (1997)

Professor of Geology and Earth Sciences

Former Clerk of the Faculty (2014-19); author of numerous scholarly papers and abstracts; writer/designer of six video games; author of one novel and two novellas

ZULFIYA TURSUNOVA (2017)

Assistant Professor of Peace and Conflict Studies

Recipient of the Bruce B. Stewart Teaching Award; author of *Women's Lives and Livelihoods in Post-Soviet Uzbekistan: Ceremonies of Empowerment and Peacebuilding* (Lexington Books, 2014)

DAVID MILLICAN (2006)

Visiting Assistant Professor of Chemistry

Author of scholarly articles and conference papers/posters; 15 years of teaching and service at Guilford

THOM ESPINOLA (1984)

Glaxo Wellcome Professor of Physics

Author of three textbooks; recipient of three NASA Grants, two Department of Education Grants, a Bryan Jr. Grant, a Kellogg Grant, and a Planetarium Grant

BOB WILLIAMS (1987)

Professor of Economics

Author of *Greening the Economy: Integrating Economics and Ecology to Make Effective Change* (Routledge, 2010)

JILL PETERFESO (2012)

Associate Professor of Religious Studies

Author of *Womanpriest: Tradition and Transgression in the Contemporary Roman Catholic Church* (Fordham University Press, 2020)

KEN GILMORE (1998)

Professor of Political Science

22 years of teaching, service, and administration at Guilford

JULIE WINTERICH (2008)

Professor of Sociology and Anthropology, Early College Liaison

Recipient of the Bruce B. Stewart Teaching Award and the Board of Visitors Award for Academic Advising; CPPS Faculty fellow; author of multiple scholarly articles and conference papers

CHAD PHILLIPS (2003)

Visiting Assistant Professor of Theatre Studies

17 years of teaching and service at Guilford

TOM GUTHRIE (2006)

Professor of Sociology and Anthropology

Author of *Recognizing Heritage: The Politics of Multiculturalism in New Mexico* (University of Nebraska Press, 2013)

Appendix 4.   Photographs.

Richie's bar mitzvah, May 1958, with his parents, Irene and Twigs. (Photo by Monte Zucker.)

Richie's bar mitzvah, May 1958, with his grandparents, Paul and Rose Stein. (Photo by Monte Zucker.)

The George School wrestling team, 1940, Grimsley Hobbs standing behind Arthur Bluethenthal, second from the right. (Photo provided by Tony Bluethenthal.)

Current and former administrators, 1984. (Photo from the Guilford College archives.) Bottom row (left to right): Cyril Harvey, Bruce Stewart, John Stoneburner; top row (left to right): Harvey Ljung, Darryl Kent, Jerry Godard, Bill Burris, Sam Schuman.

Three generations of Malino rabbis (left to right): Jerome, Tamar, and Jonathan, at Tamar's ordination in 2001. (Photo provided by Tamar Malino.)

Jonathan Malino chanting the El Maleh Rachamin for Stanley Frank, January 2005. (Photo by Nelson Kepley.)

Participants in a panel on Interfaith Dialogue on Israel/Palestine, 2014 (left to right): Rev. Jeff Paschall of Guilford Park Presbyterian Church, Max Carter, Rabbi Eli Havivi of Beth David Synagogue, and Akir Khan of the Board of the Piedmont Interfaith Council. (Photo provided by Max Carter.)

Diya Abdo, at the United Nations, 2018. (Photo by Jason Senior.)

Richie winning the Hendricks Award, with Jane Fernandes, March 2019. (Photo by Julie Knight.)

The empty chairs in front of Archdale Hall, July 2020. (Photo by Lisa McLeod.)

OKAY, GEEZERS, listen up (as my junior high school basketball coach used to say). Better yet, print this out so you can study it carefully, for there are decisions to be made.

As I mentioned in my email yesterday, I met with Brian Wenger, the Director of the athletic facility at the college. Guilford now has a system whereby we can continue to use the gym for geezer basketball. Basically, the college has rental agreements for its various facilities, and we can arrange to rent the basketball court for the days we want it. The regular fee for the Ragan-Brown Field House is $45/hour, but special discount rates (40% off) are provided for coaches and distinguished professors of psychology. This means we can rent the gym for $27 an hour. Brian assured me that we could reserve the court for an hour (say, noon to 1) but we could come earlier and stay later most of the time, and he would only charge us for the one hour. He'd like us to try to be done by 1:15 or 1:30 at the latest, so we probably will need to start by 11:30. We would reserve the court semester by semester, and either pay at the outset for the whole semester or pay by the month.

If we were to stay with our three day a week schedule, three hours a week over a 17-week semester at $27 an hour means a cost of $1377. If we were to switch to two days a week, it would come to $918. First question for you to think about is what days we should reserve. I have three options for you to consider: the traditional Monday, Wednesday, Friday; Tuesday and Thursday; or, option number 3, Tuesday, Thursday and Friday.

Second question is whether you're willing to pony up an initial fee that would put your name on the list to gain access to the gym. Brian plans to have that list at the front desk, and only people on the list will be allowed downstairs during the time we've rented the gym. Others who have legitimate access to the facility, such as students, staff and other faculty, will be directed to the upstairs gym during the time we've rented the field house. Those without legitimate access to the facility will not be allowed in. At some point "membership" cards may be issued, but it's not clear when that will happen. There is no plan to provide towels, which Brian tells me seem to disappear at alarming rates, so the bring your own towel policy will remain in effect.

The current, working, geezer list (see below) has about 30 names on it, but some of the people on the list have not been seen for a while. How much we end up paying will in part be determined by the number of geezers who sign on. For the time being, I'm suggesting an initial payment of $150 per person. If 15 people sign on, that's $2250, which covers our monthly fees well beyond December, and means I don't have to keep asking for smaller amounts (I'm not asking Guilford faculty to pay this fee, since use of the gym is one of the many, many benefits for employees here at Guilford College). As for "membership," I'm planning to start with the geezer email list and see how many sign on. We'll then decide if we want or need more people. My sense is that we'll have enough.

I'm sure that there will be decisions to make along the way about membership and other matters. My plan is to make these decisions myself, unless I want or need help. If I do, then I will draw on a Guilford College Interdisciplinary Basketball-Playing Faculty Kitchen Cabinet consisting of Thom Espinola (physics), Claire Morse (psychology) and Bob Williams (economics). In addition, I'm assuming that at times, I'll poll all paying members (to decide, for example, whether to include a new person in the game, or, just to come up with a wild example, whether to ban someone who makes the mistake of starting a fight or throwing the ball in someone's face).

Brian also said we would either need a liability policy of $1 million, or we would each need to sign a form waiving liability. I told him the latter seemed to make more sense to me, and I have copies of the form each of you will need to sign.

Okay, so here's what you need to do. First, let me know what your preferences are for game days (this you could do by email). Second, send a check made out to me for $150 (Richie Zweigenhaft, Psychology Dept., Guilford College, Greensboro, NC 27410). When I get your check, I'll either send you a copy of the waiver form through the mail, or I'll slip one to you in the locker room, though let me stress that I don't really want to conduct the business of this operation in the locker room or on the court. Brian would like to move to this system in July, perhaps before they spend a few weeks working on the floor, but maybe after they have done the floor.

Here's the working list of geezers, based on the list I sent Brian Wenger a few months back, and the email list I'm currently using (note that I have emails for most, but not all of the people on the list). If you know of regular players who are not on the list and you think they should be, let me know.

Brian Allen	Dan Lenze
Mike Brown	Greg Mayer
Craig Chappelow	Danny McCoy
Odell Cleveland	Claire Morse
Nathan Cook	Robert Pearse
George Cox	David Ratclifte
Thom Espinola	Steve Reid
Frank Hatchett	Charlie Richmond
Rusty Hoffman	Darryl Rollandelli
Ron Irons	Steve Schlehuser
Charlie Johnson	Jerrold Wheeler
Lyn Keller	Bob Williams
Steve Lemberg	Bob Wineburg
Mark Lewis	Richie Zweigenhaft
Rob Luisana	

Appendix 6. Articles About the Geezer Game and Dead Men Dribbling

Appendix 6A. "Guilford's Noontime Basketball" by Claire Morse [2]

"LET'S GO, IT'S TIME for the Committee Meeting." The meeting is indicated on the Correspondence Center schedule forms of some of us, and the admonition might be heard Monday, Wednesday, or Friday in several faculty offices. This committee meets more often than others—and it is much more enjoyable, too. On our way over to the gym, Richie and I are as likely to be discussing teaching or Guilford business as anything else. We stop only on entering our separate locker rooms. As basketballs bounce on the wooden Alumni Gym floor, the noises of warming up are mixed with greetings, heckling and business. Not just any business, more Guilford College business. After all, lots of the players are Guilford faculty or staff. Others are current Guilford students, some are graduates. Yet others are members of the Y. This committee has met faithfully at noontime on Monday, Wednesday and Friday for the last eight years. Members may serve repeated terms, and several leaves of absence have been granted. Membership is open, requiring only that one enjoy playing basketball. Skills are desirable, but not mandatory. Student eligibility also is unlimited by years or academic standing. Attendance is not officially recorded, although infrequent attendance will almost certainly be noted, and heckling may result. Tardiness is often costly—if there is not an odd number of players, or the game has already begun, the late player will probably have to wait to play. The character of this game might be captured by noting the number of players who do not know the score at any time, and by the perhaps even

2. Morse, Claire. 1985. "The Committee Meeting: Guilford's Noontime Basketball." *Guilford Review* 22(Fall):19.

larger number who do not remember who won the previous meeting day (or perhaps even later that afternoon).

The scheduled meeting time is 12:00. Actually, we usually begin playing after 12:15. It is difficult to break up the business meetings going on during the warm-up period. It is far more arduous to make up teams. Although only a few players are willing to suggest teams, all have an interest in establishing the team membership. We play competitively, and evenly matched teams make the games more interesting. Moreover, there are some match-ups to be avoided as too likely to produce dispute. Friction between players diminishes the enjoyment—and the playing time—for everyone. Even though people are reluctant to suggest teams, if someone doesn't do so, most will urge that we get started. Someone, or several people, will eventually designate the "skins" and "shirts." In spite of numerous jokes and offers, I have always been a "shirt." There may be some joking remarks about unfair teams, but they never last long.

The unwritten rules of this game commit us to seeing that everyone who comes gets a chance to play. We will divide into two games rather than requiring that a group of players wait for winners of the first game. Our game has grown over the years so that having two games is not unusual now, and having available both the Alumni Gym court and a court in the new field house is a wonderful luxury. This year we have frequently had enough for two full-court, four-on-four games, and even two five-on-five games—20 players—a few times. These crowds represent steady growth from the days when three-on-three was the typical committee meeting.

I am fairly sure that my presence has raised a few (male) eyebrows. I am the only woman who has played regularly. Sometimes a woman student or a couple of women from the basketball team have joined our game, but this has been rare. And one noon we played against the Guilford women's team. Apparently Coach Currie wanted the women to see how aggressively the game can be played. Being the only woman has always been interesting. Initially I was quite nervous, both about how well I could play and whether the men would include me in the game when I was on the court. That feeling diminished as I had a few successful games, and I acquired a certain measure of longevity, not to mention seniority. (By now, at 42, I am one of the oldest players). I think that the men make some adjustments to the presence of a woman. For example, I think there is hesitation on the part of new players about what sort of language is acceptable in this game. Some players never seem to express emotional responses in "four letter words," and some men have apologized to me for their word choice; however, since I use some foul words myself, I think that at least frees most of the men from the injunction prohibiting cursing around women and permits a release of frustration with a loud expletive on the part of other players, I am also not the only one who groans or chides myself for a missed shot or poor play. I do shout in unhappiness more than most, and was warned before going to U Mass on a study leave three years ago not to do that there. I did, and again found that there were a few others who also did. But few.

Physical contact and fouling can lead to conflict in any pickup game, and they sometimes do at the Committee Meeting. We each call fouls committed against us, and frequently we call those we commit on another player. I sometimes sense that my male opponents will call fouls against themselves when those infractions are committed on me which they would not call if their opponent were another male. And sometimes men apologize to me for incidental contact. But then, I apologize to them for the same sort of thing. Perhaps the reciprocity which I value—I'll try to call my fouls fairly and I will expect you to do likewise—is best established that way. It seems a generally shared attitude during our meetings. I do despise losing the ball to superior male upper body muscle strength, but it happens and seems inevitable. I do not mind being sent flying by some simple collision with a heavier player since I view that as part of playing the game, and have never sensed that any of the other players were malicious or intent on causing injury. Unaware of other players, perhaps, but not mean.

I'd like to know more about what the game has meant to other players. For me it has provided wonderful exercise with a group of people including some whom I would otherwise not know or spend time with. These men are comrades of a special sort, and our shared play can certainly lead me to respect and enjoy them from the perspective of a woman who has been allowed to participate simply as another player in a game we all enjoy. The game has provided me the basis for further appreciation of several members of the Guilford College community who are fun to play ball with, and who bring basketball talents one might not have expected from being at other committee meetings together. The contact with students has also been of a special sort. Student players have been numerous over the years, if not quite as regular as others. The chance to play with or against a student who is or has been in one of my classes is a special opportunity to see him (rarely her) moving fast, shooting well, and beating a professor to a rebound. There is humbling, there is winning, there is joking. I've not sensed gloating or belittling. I know that students know about the noontime game, and they must therefore realize that a group of men and women, from high school to "middle age," can play decent basketball and take great delight in it. After all the faculty members of the Committee Meeting have always played better than .500 ball in the intramural league.

The Committee Meeting continues, we welcome new players, and anticipate steady growth in numbers. Perhaps a new field house?

Appendix 6B. "Order on the Court: A Lesson in Leadership" by Craig Chappelow[3]

IN THESE DAYS of jargon-filled mission statements, it is refreshing to find an example of a leader walking the talk. I am lucky that I get to see an example of this mission clarity every week. All I have to do is pick up my sneakers and head out of the office at lunchtime. At the Guilford College YMCA in my hometown of Greensboro, North Carolina, there is a group of people who spend the lunch hour playing in a pickup basketball game. Nothing particularly unusual about that—except that this lunch game started twenty-four years ago and is still going strong. Group members have come and gone over the years, but a steady core of banged-up, liniment-covered hasbeens continue to strap on their high-tops and go at it as if the NBA title were at stake. For the thirty or so men and women who play regularly, it is the highlight of the week. Our mission statement, if we had one, would be something like this: "Get exercise."

The group is a hodgepodge of former jocks and nonathletes from all professions. Last week my teammates consisted of an engineer, a podiatrist, an artist, and a guy who collects tractors. All of us have one thing in common. We depend on being able to show up, get into a game quickly, get some exercise, take a shower, and get back to work before anyone notices we were gone.

Keeper of the Flame

HOW IS IT that this particular game has endured for twenty-four years? A great deal of the credit must go to the leader, Richie Zweigenhaft. It is easy to overlook Richie because he is usually

3. Chappelow, Craig. 2000. "Order on the Court: A Lesson in Leadership." *Leadership in Action* 20(5):13-14.

the smallest player on the court. With his oversized safety goggles, headband, long shorts, high socks, and bushy beard, he looks more like a psychology professor than like a ballplayer. That's probably because he is a psychology professor—more Carl Jung than Karl Malone. It was Richie who, together with a handful of other Guilford College faculty members, started this pickup game twenty-four years ago, and it is Richie who consistently walks the talk.

I have learned some important things about leadership from watching Richie. Most of these tips are things that I think any leader could apply to his or her work:

Be clear about your mission. The mission for our group is to get a workout. Everything else comes second. Years ago, Richie and the other charter members established a system of rotating players in and out of the games and across the courts to reduce the amount of time people have to wait to play. Even if you show up late, you will be rotated into a game within a few minutes.

Don't waste your team members' time. Everyone who plays in the noon league has a limited amount of time at lunch. That means that chitchat about last night's football game on TV or a discussion of departmental politics must wait. By modeling this kind of focus, Richie has transmitted this priority to the other players. He is a nice guy, but if you try to indulge in small talk with him between games, he'll politely shrug you off as he gets the next game under way. This is not out of rudeness but rather is in service to the mission. Another professor in Richie's department at Guilford College who is a regular lunch league player, Claire Morse, says Richie's off-court leadership behaviors are similar: "He is well prepared for his responsibilities and takes them seriously, but he finds ways to enjoy them too. He makes other people's lives better in the process."

Confront problems swiftly but selectively and calmly. The majority of the players in the noon league are middle-age folks well on the downhill side of their sports skills—if they had any such skills to begin with. There are enough spare tires on the court to outfit a tractor-trailer. Even so, the games can get highly competitive. When an argument breaks out between two players, Richie quietly changes the defensive assignments. This separates the two players and reduces the chance of further problems. Richie doesn't try to mediate between the players or reach a resolution. That would detract from the mission. Bob Wineburg, a professor of social work at the University of North Carolina at Greensboro and a longtime league member, describes Richie's problem-solving style this way: "He doesn't lecture; he makes strategic moves." In my thirteen years of playing in the league I have seen Richie annoyed, frustrated, and discouraged but never angry.

Seek fairness and balance. Everyone looks to Richie to divide the players into teams to get the games started—not because the rest of us can't but because Richie has an uncanny knack for setting up balanced teams. Dan McCoy, a mortgage banker and lunch league regular, points out that "Richie would enjoy nothing more than a three-game split with the scores 15 to 13. As some of us approach our fifth decade, if not for Richie's influence on the noon game we would be forced to abandon the game we love."

Lead by example. Ralph Waldo Emerson is credited with saying, "What you do speaks so loudly that I cannot hear what you say." Richie doesn't say much, but his actions say a great deal. If we have to stop a competitive game and send two players to the next court to fill out teams to start a second game, Richie will go. He would rather pass the ball than shoot—although he shoots well. Most of all he doesn't do anything that doesn't serve the mission of the group.

Appendix 6c. "Men Score at Senior Games" by Rob Luisana[4]

WHILE WE ENTERED the Senior Game basketball game competition under the team name, Dead Men Dribbling, we were actually Geezer basketball players. That is, the group of older basketball players who had migrated to Guilford College to play in the lunch time basketball games that were held there, three days a week.

For myself and many of the other players, it had been a long road to Geezer basketball, covering basketball courts from what was called the Rocket ship park on Market Street in the 70's, to the games outdoors at Lake Daniels Park, to the First Baptist Church, to the small outdoor court at College Park, to the Central YMCA, to Sportime and finally to the Guilford College Gym. Most players are over 40, a few over 55, the qualifying age to play in the North Carolina Senior Games.

When Bob Wineburg, one of the Geezer basketball players, told several of us Geezers that he had been diagnosed with cancer, all of us were amazed at the courage and humor with which he approached the disease. I had played basketball with and against Bob for years at Guilford College, and we'd known one another as neighbors in the Aycock neighborhood before that. When he told me about his diagnosis of cancer, I tried to think of ways to cheer him, and the one thing that I knew would get him excited was the idea of competition.

After his surgery, I visited with him while he was recovering. We walked slowly around his block and talked about playing basketball in the Senior Games. In spite of his pain, he was clearly excited about the idea.

I had thought about playing in the Senior Games before Bob's illness pushed me to sign up. Part of the reason to play was

4. Luisana, Rob. 2006. "Men Score at Senior Games." *News & Record*, January 16, 10–12.

to fight back against getting older. I was 56, not only receiving literature from AARP, but old enough to join. Turning 30, 40 and 50 hadn't fazed me; somehow, 55 was more of a milestone. Maybe playing in a basketball tournament was one way to fight the fact that I was getting older.

Certainly there aren't many 55-and-older ball players left—injuries and just plain wear and tear take a toll. Many of my friends quit playing basketball saying, "I just got tired of hurting all the time." Over the past 20 years, I had racked up an assortment of injuries. Broken foot, which put me on crutches for a month. Broken nose, bad enough to have it reset. My wife, Karen, had pushed hard for getting the nose reset. Finally, a compartment injury to my left calf. My list of injuries is not unusual for someone who plays competitive basketball for 40 years. Many Geezer players list a similar assortment of injuries.

When we played against each other, Wineburg complained often and loudly about the way I played, claiming that I was fouling or going over his back to get to the ball or generally being too competitive. But he wanted to win every basketball game we played and was probably the most competitive of all of us Geezers. With Wineberg and myself, we were still at least 3 players short of a team. The Senior Games are half-court, three-on-three and we needed at least two substitutes.

We were desperate for a big man. I knew, I didn't want to be the designated big man, since I'm 6'1" and weigh 185 pounds. Unfortunately there was no big man around. Knees and other body parts essential to playing basketball begin to wear out after 30 and that is especially true for bigger players.

We recruited the best three over-55 Geezers available. Next on board was Richie Zweigenhaft, all 5-foot-7 and 130 pounds. Smart player, unselfish, good shooter and passer and already established as the preeminent Geezer leader. Not because he was the best player, but because he was always trying to do what was right. He was allowed to pick the teams and did so fairly. To promote sportsmanship and to make everyone feel good, he even admonished us to no longer refer to our oldest player as "old Steve" but as "Steve the Elder." He was going to be a member of the team as much for his ability to stay level-headed as for his basketball skills.

Our next recruit was Lynn Keller, a strong player. Best one-on-one player we had. Excellent shooter from 15 feet to 18 feet and able to drive to the basket, take a foul and still make the shot; rebounded well for his size, 5 foot 10, and always played hard. He packed the most immaculate gym bag I had ever seen.

Our final player was Charlie Johnson, who at 6-foot-1 is an excellent shooter and a smart player. He created shots for himself by constant movement. Of the five of us, Charlie was the only local boy. He played high school basketball at Southeast High in the 60's. Charlie played to win and often got into arguments over his willingness to foul rather than to give up an easy shot. His size and toughness would help us on the boards and offset some of my weaknesses.

When it became known that we would play in the Senior Games some Geezer players predicted how we would do. Probably the most telling scouting report came from Danny McCoy, who wrote in an email analysis of the team: "Strong offense, limited rebounding, really strong on rule interpretation."

I had given little thought to how well we would fit together as teammates, assuming five senior citizens could coexist and play together without a problem. But one day, after we finished playing and showering, I heard loud, angry noises coming from the locker room.

I walked out to find teammates Charlie Johnson and Bob Wineburg screaming at one another, faces 10 inches apart. The source of the argument was, incredibly, George Bush's speech on Social Security and tax policy. This was new ground for me.

In 40-plus years of playing basketball, I heard and witnessed plenty of locker room arguments, along with a few fights, all of which involved either a girl or another player's unwillingness to share the basketball. This was the first time I'd seen two basketball players preparing to come to blows over tax policy.

I walked into the locker room and looked at Bob Williams, who was laughing. I said, "Well, do you think the team is going to have chemistry problems?" He responded, "Look at the players on the team and tell me how you're not going to have problems." The Senior Games were uncharted territory for all of us.

The guidelines to participate in the Games required that we play several practice games with a referee and under the official Senior Games rules. Our first scrimmage game was set against some of the younger Geezer players who had not yet reached the qualifying age-55 mark. Despite not having Charlie Johnson, who was injured, and being at a clear height disadvantage, we won two out of three games.

The second series of practice games came against the 60–65 age team from Winston-Salem. The games were competitive, and the Winston-Salem team would go on to win the State in their division. We won all 3 games and began to actually think we would be a factor when we went to Greenville in October.

We arrived at the ECU student center for the Saturday morning opening ceremonies along with teams from across North Carolina. The competition was divided into age brackets for men's and women's teams. The youngest bracket was ages 55-59. There would be 16 men's teams and eight women's teams in this age group. The number of teams dropped with each bracket. Twelve teams competed in the 60-65 men's bracket, three in the women's group. The oldest team from Orange County competed in the 80 and above men's division, the only team entered. Longevity has its rewards.

Our first game was against the Pitt County team. While we had the shortest team in the competition, they had the tallest. Despite the size disadvantage, we led for most of the first half and went into the halftime break down by only three points. We ended up losing by nine points.

We won the second game easily by 20 points. Lynn and Charlie led the scoring, but everyone played well.

The competition was divided into pools of four or five teams with the top two teams from each pool advancing to the quarterfinals.

Our third game against a team from Western Carolina would determine if we advanced.

The Western Carolina team was almost as big as the Pitt County team, definitely physical. The game was close with neither team able to generate more than a five-point lead. There was a great deal of shoving and fouling, much never called by the referees.

Our lack of size and bulk hurt us, as well as the fact that we couldn't stop their best player, who must have scored 75 percent of their points. The game ended with a three-point loss.

We wouldn't advance to play Sunday. Still, there was something worthwhile about being there. It was certainly inspiring to watch men and women 20 years older than us out on the basketball court continuing to compete.

POSTSCRIPT: Deadmen Dribbling returned to the Senior Games again this past October and with the addition of Tally Mitchell as a player and Frank Hatchett as coach managed to win two out of three games in their pool.

They're still looking for an over-55 post player.

Appendix 6D. "The Geezer Game and Dead Men Dribbling" by Richie Zweigenhaft [5]

I USED TO THINK that our mid-day geezer basketball game here at Guilford was unique. Three days a week, a bunch of us, now ranging in age from 40-65, play five-on-five full court basketball at Guilford College. The game began back in 1976, in the old gym (Alumni Gym), known then by all as "the crackerbox." For many years, we called the game "the committee meeting" so that when actual committees we were on tried to schedule meetings during our sacred basketball time, we'd say that we couldn't meet then because had another meeting scheduled.

Many who have played in our game through the years have retired or moved away, but here we are, 30 years later, still playing, three days a week, full court, most days in Ragan-Brown, but some days in Alumni Gym. The game, now known (affectionately, but also officially) as "the geezer game," consists of faculty, staff and a bunch of guys who used to be YMCA members when the college had an affiliation with the Y, and who now pay dues to rent the court three times a week (I used to be known as Rockaday Johnny, but now some call me "the commissioner"). Hung on the rafters are imaginary banners with the imaginary retired numbers of former participants, such as John "Radar" Stoneburner, Mel "Truck" Keiser, and Ken "Indiana Hook Shot" Schwab.

Our game probably is unique, in the same way that no two snowflakes, no two people, and no two pickup basketball games are exactly the same. But now that a subgroup of our geezer game has competed in a statewide three-on-three half court tournament at East Carolina University (ECU) that is part of

5. Zweigenhaft, Richie. 2006. "The Geezer Game and Dead Men Dribbling." (http://class.guilford.edu/pages/modules/10000/depts/psychology/richie/bball.htm)

something called "The Senior Games," I realize that there are geezers throughout North Carolina still putting up jumpers, 1950's-style hook shots, and occasional air balls.

Our team ("Dead Men Dribbling") was one of 16 teams entered in the 55-59-year-old bracket. I was surprised that there were so many teams at that advanced age (well, I'm closer to 62 than to 61, but I was "playing down"). I was even more surprised that there were 12 men's teams in the 60-64-year-old bracket, a bunch of teams in the 65-69-year-old bracket, some in the 70-74 and 74-79 year old brackets, and, get this, two teams in the over-80 bracket. There were also women's teams, ranging in age from 55 to 75. In short, for one autumn weekend the fancy new sports palace at ECU, clearly built to attract virile young college students, was filled with geezers who still play basketball.

So how'd we do? Well, in the first game we played a team from Pinehurst ("Pinehurst Hip and Knee Bobcats"), the first of three games we were to play against opponents who were bigger than we were at each position every minute of every game. Though we were smaller, we were also quicker, and we played well. In the last minute of the game, we lost the small lead we had been holding, but we then eked out a win on a shot with three seconds left by 59-year-old Lyn Keller. An hour later, in game two, against a team called "Hoopsters," from somewhere in North Carolina, but I'm not sure where, we jumped to a lead midway through the first half, which we kept, winning by 14 points. As time began to wind down in the second half, the Hoopsters began to foul us as soon as we passed the ball in, and we spent a lot of time at the foul line. Bob Wineburg, now 56, but who at the age of 14 won the city-wide junior high school foul shooting championship in Utica, New York, drilled a series of foul shots; it was the calmest any of us had seen Wineburg in years.

Game three turned out to be another story. We played a team from Charlotte ("Never too Late")—their pre-game rep was that one of their many good, big, players is the brother of Walter Davis, former UNC and NBA star (Walter, not the brother). They made our "big" men (57-year-old Rob Luisana, 6'1", our team captain, and 56-year-old Tally Mitchell, also 6'1"), look small. But, they had lost to the Pinehurst Hip and Knee Bobcats, the team we had beaten in our first game, so we assumed we could beat them. Maybe we could, but not that day. We stayed close for a while, trailing by four at the half. But they were big, they managed to get the ball inside to their big men, we kept fouling them, and they kept hitting their foul shots. (Unbecoming and whiny as it sounds, we were getting clobbered and fouls were not called. Unlike in the first two games, when our quickness got us to the foul line a lot, we barely got to the foul line in this game, though we should have). The bottom fell out midway through the second half when Never Too Late began to drain three-point shots—they must have hit six or seven in a five-minute span. We got clobbered. (We do not blame this loss on our coach, Frank Hatchett, a regular participant in the geezer game but who, at a mere 42 years of age, is much too young to play on Dead Men Dribbling. Coach Hatchett, who drove down that morning from Greensboro to coach us, last year coached the junior varsity at Greensboro Day to a 31-1 record. Therefore, our 2-1 record lowered his lifetime winning percentage. Neither John Wooden nor Dean Smith could have saved us in game three).

Three of the four teams in our bracket went 2-1 (the other was 0-3), but only two could move on to play in the next round the next morning. Because this was determined by point differential, and because we lost our third game 48-32, we were out. As it turned out, our bracket-mates did well: "Never Too

The next year, we win bronze.

Late" came in second in the tournament, and the "Pinehurst Hip and Knee Bobcats" came in third.

Tired and hungry, we ate dinner, during which we went over every play of each of the three games, and then drove back to Greensboro, talking about next year.

Appendix 6E. "Geezer game: Playing together for 31 years" by Robert Bell[6]

IT'S LUNCHTIME on a sunny December afternoon when the game begins at Guilford College's Ragan-Brown Field House. Outside, a warm spell has pushed the temperature close to 60, and lovers walk hand-in hand across the campus. Inside, there's a different romance going on: Ten guys going at it in a game of full-court basketball, which would be unremarkable except they're all old enough to be somebody's grandfather.

Some guys hit their 50s or 60s and take up golf. Others, the only exercise they manage is lifting themselves from the dinner table.

The guys at Ragan-Brown show up three times a week and run up and down the court for more than an hour, knowing it's a cheap, wonderful tonic for the ravages of old age.

"I always wondered what I'd be doing when I got, you know, closer to retirement," says Dan McCoy, 56 and a regular in the so-called "geezer game" each week. "This was not what I thought I'd be doing."

Yet here he is playing basketball with a dozen or so other middle-aged guys who love the game and can't give it up. The guys (and gals) include Richie Zweigenhaft, 62, who started these pickup games 31 years ago; Bob Wineburg, 57 and cancer-free for five years now; and Claire Morse, 62, who grew up playing the game way back when and has been unable to shake its pull since.

Watch them for a while and you see this is the basketball of pick-and-rolls, hook shots, two-handed set shots and running one-handers. This is basketball from another era, the game set in sepia. This is basketball before ESPN. Before the between-

6. Bell, Robert. 2007. "Geezer Game: Playing Together for 31 Years." *News & Record*, December 22. (https://www.greensboro.com/sports/geezer-game/article_5e1ff224-afa2-57c4-92f2-72ca69951b62.html)

the-legs dribbling and the monster dunks of today's game—even before the jump shot, really.

"It's the game we grew up with," says 58-year-old Rob Luisana, another player. "It's the only one we know." Zweigenhaft says younger guys are allowed to play, provided they adhere to two rules: They must pass the ball, and they must be willing to play defense. "That usually eliminates a lot of guys," Zweigenhaft says. "But some catch on and enjoy it. It's like a whole new game has opened up to them."

Frank Hatchett, 46, took his game to Guilford College when his health club closed a few years back. He started for three years at Greensboro Day School, where he was an all-state player. He figured he could teach the old guys some new tricks. "I found out quickly they weren't pushovers," Hatchett says. "My first game with them I was thinking: Hey, these guys actually pass to each other. They cut through the lane. They're constantly looking for the open man."

Zweigenhaft says: "We play a different game than the one they play on the street nowadays."

And they play it well. Last month, five of the players finished third at the North Carolina Senior Games, playing three-on-three half-court basketball.

Zweigenhaft, a psychology professor at Guilford, organized the first pickup game in 1976 at Alumni Gym, affectionately known on campus as the "crackerbox" where Lloyd Free and M.L. Carr played for the Quakers.

The pickup players consisted of Guilford faculty and former YMCA members (the school once was affiliated with the Spears YMCA). Thirty-one years later, some guys have moved, some have retired and a few have died, but the geezer game is going strong every Monday, Wednesday and Friday—Sundays at Grimsley High School if the guys have any energy left.

Bob Wineburg (right) guards Richie Zweigenhaft (left) during a basketball game at Guilford College in Greensboro, NC, Friday, December 21, 2007.

Thirty-one years is a long time for anything. Even Zweigenhaft is surprised the games have endured. "There's been a whole new generation of players who have come in and stayed with it," he says. "I don't think it's the competition that keeps guys (coming back) as much as it is the camaraderie." As the group's self-proclaimed commissioner, Zweigenhaft annually nominates someone for comeback player of the year. Four years ago, Wineburg seemed a lock for the award because he was recovering from prostate cancer. Instead, he lost out to 66-year-old Steve Schlehuser, who nearly died on the operating table that year. "We play through our injuries," Zweigenhaft jokes.

Many of the players say they feel the pain of their games when they get back to work. But none of them is about to trade in those aches for a rocking chair.

"My wife says she expects to get a call one day saying I've died on the basketball court," McCoy says. "If that happens, she'll know I died happy."

References

Abdo, Diya. 2015. "Sayf," in *27 Views of Greensboro: The Gate City in Prose and Poetry*, Hillsborough, NC: Eno Publishers), pp. 47–53.

Abdo, Diya. 2015. "The most valuable lesson from Steven Salaita's visit to Guilford College," *The Electronic Intifada*, February 5; https://electronicintifada.net/content/most-valuable-lesson-steven-salaitas-visit-guilford-college/14246

Abunimah, Ali. 2015. "North Carolina college bows to donor over Steven Salaita talk," *The Electronic Intifada*, February 2; https://electronicintifada.net/blogs/ali-abunimah/north-carolina-college-bows-donor-pressure-over-steven-salaita-talk

Appenzeller, Herb. 1987. *Pride in the Past*, Greensboro, NC: Guilford College.

Baker, Jean H. 1997. *The Stevensons: A Biography*, New York: W. W. Norton.

Baker, Peter. 2018. "Was Jimmy Carter the Most Underrated President in History?" *New York Times*, June 5. https://www.nytimes.com/2018/06/05/books/review/president-carter-stuart-eizenstat.html

Barnes, Bart. 2018. "Landrum Bolling, college president, peace activist and presidential go-between dies at 104," *Washington Post*, January 30; https://www.washingtonpost.com/local/obituaries/landrum-bolling-college-president-peace-activist-and-presidential-go-between-dies-at-104/2018/01/30/2f0a1060-053a-11e8-8777-2a059f168dd2_story.html

Bauman, Dan. 2020. "Colleges Have Shed a Tenth of Their Employees Since the Pandemic Began," *Chronicle of Higher Education*, November 10, 2020. https://www.chronicle.com/article/colleges-have-shed-a-tenth-of-their-employees-since-the-pandemic-began

Beal, Gertrude and Max Carter. 2019. *Stories from a Quaker Graveyard*. Greensboro, NC: The New Garden Cemetery Association.

Belkin, Douglas. 2020. "Hit by Covid, Colleges do the Unthinkable and Cut Tenure," *Wall Street Journal*, December 6, 2020. https://www.wsj.com/articles/hit-by-covid-19-colleges-do-the-unthinkable-and-cut-tenure-11607250780

Bell, Robert. 2007. "Geezer game: Playing together for 31 years," *News & Record*, December 22. https://www.greensboro.com/sports/geezer-game/article_5e1ff224-afa2-57c4-92f2-72ca69951b62.html

Benfey, Christopher. 2012. *Red Brick, Black Mountain, White Clay: Reflections on Art, Family, & Survival*, New York: Penguin.

Bolling, Landrum R. 1968. "What Chance for Peace in the Middle East," *Friends Journal: Quaker Thought and Life Today*, September 1, pp. 430- 433.

Bolling, Landrum R. 1970. *Search for Peace in the Middle East*, Philadelphia, PA: American Friends Service Committee.

Bourdieu, Pierre. 1986. "The Forms of Capital," pp. 241– 58 in *Handbook of theory and research for the sociology of education*, edited by J. G. Richardson. New York: Greenwood Press.

Carter, Jimmy. 2016. "American Must Recognize Palestine," *New York Times*, November 29, A27.

Carter, Max L. and Jonathan W. Malino. 2015. "More than 2 stories in Israel, Palestine," *News & Record*, February 8. https://www.greensboro.com/more-than-2-stories-in-israel-palestine/article_181f584c-e716-588d-a773-c603def6d7a7.html

Carter, Max L. 2020. *Palestine and Israel: A Personal Encounter*, Newberg, OR: Barclay Press.

Chace, William. 1980. *Civilities and Civil Rights. Greensboro, North Carolina, and the Black Struggle for Freedom*. Oxford University Press.

Chappelow, Craig. 2000. "Order on the Court: A Lesson in Leadership," *Leadership in Action*, 20 (5), pp. 14–15.

Coe, Kathy. 1990. "Grimsley T. Hobbs," *News & Record*. November 20. https://www.greensboro.com/grimsley-t-hobbs/article_6983d53d-77ae-586f-b1b2-9cf747546d39.html

Daniels, Wess. 2008. "Quaker Voting Poll, 2008." https://www.slideshare.net/cwdaniels/quaker-voting-presentation

Diaz-Cepeda, Luis Ruben, and Ernesto Castañeda. 2019. "Activists' Motivations and Typologies: Core Activists in Ciudad Juárez," *Interface* 11:1: 89-122 (July, 2019).

Domhoff, G. William. 1990. *The Power Elite and the State: How Policy is Made in America*, New York: Aldine de Gruyter.

Dreier, Peter. 2020. "Martin Luther King Jr., the Civil Rights Movement, and American Jews," *Los Angeles Review of Books*, January 18. https://lareviewofbooks.org/article/martin-luther-king-jr-the-civil-rights-movement-and-american-jews/

Eppsteiner, Ty. 2001. "A Farewell to Joe Groves," *The Guilfordian*, April 13. https://www.guilfordian.com/archives/2001/04/13/a-farewell-to-joe-groves/

Erickson, Gwen. 2007. "Guilford College," in *Founded by Friends: The Quaker Heritage of Fifteen American Colleges and Universities*, edited by John W. Oliver, Jr., Charles L. Cherry, and Caroline L. Cherry (21-42). Lanham, MD: The Scarecrow Press.

Erickson, Gwen. "Race Relations at Guilford College," Digital Collections, UNCG. http://libcdm1.uncg.edu/cdm/essayguilford/collection/CivilRights

Fager, Chuck. 2020. "A Catholic Reckoning? How About an Evangelical Quaker Reckoning?" *A Friendly Letter*, April 28. https://afriendlyletter.com/a-catholic-reckoning-how-about-an-evangelical-quaker-reckoning/#more-15941

Flaherty, Colleen. 2021. "'A Watershed Moment' for Shared Governance," *Inside Higher Ed*, May 26, 2021. https://www.insidehighered.com/news/2021/05/26/aaup-finds-major-erosion-shared-governance-during-covid-19

Grimes, Tom. 2010. *Mentor: A Memoir*. Portland, OR: Tin House.

Guanhua, Wang. 2003. "'Friendship First': China's Sports Diplomacy in the Cold War Era," *Journal of American-East Asian Relations* 12 (3-4), pp. 133-153.

Halbfinger, David, Michael Wines, and Steven Erlanger. 2019. "A Look at the International Drive to Boycott Israel," *New York Times*, July 28, Section A8.

Hamm, Thomas, "Landrum Bolling: Advocate for Peace," Earlham College Special Collections. https://earlham.edu/media/2940505/Landrum-Bolling-obituary.pdf

Isaacs, Stephen D. 1974. *Jews in American Politics*, Garden City, NY: Doubleday.

Jarboe, Michelle. 2006. "'Advocate' Laid to Rest." *Greensboro News & Record*, January 5. https://www.greensboro.com/news/advocate-laid-to-rest/article_76fe8803-1ece-52f2-93d2-684413459777.html

Jaschik, Scott. 2015. "Guilford moves lecture by Steven Salaita," *Inside Higher Education*, February 3. https://www.insidehighered.com/quicktakes/2015/02/03/guilford-moves-lecture-steven-salaita

Jasper, James. 1997. *The Art of Moral Protest*, Chicago: University of Chicago Press.

Klatch, Rebecca E. 1999. *A Generation Divided: The New Left, The New Right, and the 1960s*, Berkeley, CA: University of California Press.

Linfield, Susie. 2019. *The Lions' Den: Zionism and the Left from Hannah Arendt to Noam Chomsky*. New Haven: Yale University Press.

Lofton, Bonnie Price. 2001. "AU's Peace Institute 2001: Practice, Scholarship, and Development," *Peacebuilder*, Issue 2014-2015. https://emu.edu/now/peacebuilder/2015/07/aus-peace-institute-2001-practice-scholarship-and-development/

Luisana, Rob. 2007. "Men Score at Senior Games," *News & Record*, January 16, pp. 10 and 12; https://www.greensboro.com/life/community_news/men-score-at-senior-games/article_3228569d-33a5-50fd-a509-89d0cd3df636.html

Mackey, Robert. 2014. "Professor's Angry Tweets on Gaza Cost Him a Job," *New York Times*, September 12. https://www.nytimes.com/2014/09/13/world/middleeast/professors-angry-tweets-on-gaza-cost-him-a-job.html

McCaughey, Martha and Michael D. Ayers (Eds.). 2003. *Cyberactivism: Online Activism in Theory and Practice*, New York: Routledge.

Minsky, Sara. 2015. "Narratives About Us, By Us: Progressive Jewish Groups in the United States Combatting Corporate Media," Honors thesis, Guilford College, May, 2015.

Morse, Claire. 1985. "Guilford's Noontime Basketball," *Guilford Review*, 22 (Fall), pp. 17–19.

Nelson, Cary, and Gabriel Brahm. 2015. *The Case Against Academic Boycotts of Israel*, MLA Members for Scholars Rights.

Nelson, Cary. 2019. *Israel Denial: Anti-Zionism, Anti-Semitism, & the Faculty Campaign Against the Jewish State*, Bloomington, IN: Indiana University Press.

Newsome, John. 2020. "'Heartbreaking:' Guilford College to make deep cuts to its academic majors and faculty," *News & Record*, November 6, 2020. https://greensboro.com/news/local/education/heartbreaking-guilford-college-to-make-deep-cuts-to-its-academic-majors-and-faculty/article_7755e64e-1f88-11eb-8cf0-4743eb7847ae.html

Newsome, John. 2020. "The Syllabus: A no-confidence vote in Guilford College's Leadership." *News & Record*. November 17, 2020. https://greensboro.com/blogs/the_syllabus/the-syllabus-a-no-confidence-vote-in-guilford-colleges-leadership/article_05888894-25e8-11eb-948c-e701522dfa6e.html

Pettit, Emma. 2019. "'Ousted' from Academe, Steven Salaita Says He's Driving a School Bus to Make Ends Meet," *Chronicle of Higher Education*. February 19. https://www.chronicle.com/article/Ousted-From-Academe/245732

Podolsky, Jonathon. 2021. "Is Guilford College on track to recovery? Yes...and no." *News & Record*, July 25, 2021. https://greensboro.com/opinion/columnists/jonathon-podolsky-is-guilford-college-on-track-to-recovery-yes-and-no/article_26ecd736-e4b2-11eb-9627-bb4a32e4762a.html

Rich, Eric. 2004. "Student who hid box cutters on BWI flight gets probation," *Washington Post*, June 25. https://www.washingtonpost.com/archive/local/2004/06/25/student-who-hid-box-cutters-on-bwi-flight-gets-probation/e0e3337d-cea9-427b-b203-401d0bbf747f/

Roth, Philip. 1993. *Operation Shylock: A Confession*. New York: Simon and Schuster.

Scheer, Robert. 1993. "Lessons from a Missed Opportunity: Eyewitness: Andrew Young," *Los Angeles Times*, September 12. https://www.latimes.com/archives/la-xpm-1993-09-12-op-34888-story.html

Schlosser, Jim. 2009. "Guilford Grad Leads School Obama Girls are Attending," *News & Record*, January 13. https://www.greensboro.com/news/columnists/guilford-grad-leads-school-obama-girls-are-attending/article_6340bdf0-3bf4-5fce-bba6-6515c2324151.html

Schuman, Samuel. 2010. *Seeing the Light: Religious Colleges in the Twenty-First Century*, Baltimore, MD: Johns Hopkins University Press.

Scott, David. 1985. "Glory Days: Guilford Basketball in the 70s," *Guilford Review*, Volume 22, pp. 28-30.

Shavit, Ari. 2013. *My Promised Land: The Triumph and Tragedy of Israel*, New York: Spiegel and Grau.

Simmons, Kelly. 1993. "Two Students Charged with Indecent Exposure/Guilford College Students," *News & Record*, February 22. https://www.greensboro.com/two-charged-with-indecent-exposure-guilford-college-students/article_0575aa27-d9fe-5303-aacc-618c05aaff4f.html

Springsteen, Bruce. 2016. *Born to Run*, New York: Simon and Schuster.

Stoesen, Alex. 1987. *Guilford College: On the Strength of 150 Years*, Greensboro, NC: Guilford College.

Thorne, Dorothy Gilbert. 1937. *Guilford: A Quaker College*, Greensboro, NC: Guilford College.

Tutu, Desmond. 2014. "My Plea to the People of Israel: Liberate Yourselves by Liberating Palestine". *Haaretz*, August 14.

Warren, Trajan. 2021. "Can Guilford College survive? Confidence builds, but questions linger," *Triad Business*

Journal, June 25, 2021. https://www.bizjournals.com/triad/news/2021/06/25/can-guilford-college-survive.html

Weil, Josh. 2015. "Steven Salaita's visit promotes division in Guilford's community," *The Guilfordian*, February 6. https://www.guilfordian.com/opinion/2015/02/06/letter-to-the-editor-steven-salaitas-visit-promotes-division-in-guilfords-community/

Whitford, Emma. 2020. "Deep Budget and Program Cuts Roil Guilford," *Inside Higher Ed*, November 23, 2020. https://www.insidehighered.com/news/2020/11/23/rare-no-confidence-vote-highlights-division-over-cuts-guilford-college

Zelniker, Nicole. 2015. "How Guilford Hillel Became Guilford Chavurah," *New Voices*, May 5. https://newvoices.org/2015/05/05/how-guilford-hillel-became-guilford-chavurah/

Zweigenhaft, Richard L. 2004. "Making Rags Out of Riches: Horatio Alger and the Tycoon's Obituary," in *Extra! The Magazine of FAIR—the Media Watch Group*, 17 (1), pp. 27–28.

Zweigenhaft, Richard L. 2010. "Is This Curriculum for Sale?" *Academe*, 96 (4), 38-39. July–August, 2010. https://www.aaup.org/article/curriculum-sale-0#.W98h99VKiig

Zweigenhaft, Richard L. 2015. "Gentrification and its discontents: Forty Years in Fisher Park." In Woodman, Elizabeth (Ed.), *27 Views of Greensboro: The Gate city in Prose and Poetry*. Hillsborough, NC: Eno Publications, pp. 64–68.

Zweigenhaft, Richard L. 2017. "Studying Diversity in the American Power Structure, Collaboratively." In Zweigenhaft, R. L. and Borgida, E. (Eds.), *Collaboration in Psychological Science: Behind the Scenes*, New York: Worth, pp. 175–187.

Zweigenhaft, Richard L. 2022. "How the AAUP Helped to Save Guilford College," *Academe*. 108 (1), 39–45. https://www.aaup.org/article/how-aaup-helped-save-guilford-college#.YbIdWVXMKig

Zweigenhaft, Richard L. and Eugene Borgida (Eds.). 2017. *Collaboration in Psychological Science: Behind the Scenes,* New York: Worth.

Zweigenhaft, Richard L. and G. William Domhoff. 1982. *Jews in the Protestant Establishment.* New York: Praeger.

Acknowledgments

In reverse alphabetical order:

LISA YOUNG, for the invaluable critique of early drafts, and for so much more.

ADELE WAYMAN, for her willingness to share with me the complex story of how being Jewish fit in her lifetime of creative exploration.

DAVE WALTERS, Sports Information Director extraordinaire, for his help with sports data throughout the years, including some that landed in *GEEZERBALL*.

RICK VOIGT, for listening to me talk about the Geezerball project, but mainly I thank him so that he won't be too miffed about what I wrote about lawyers.

JON VARNELL, for the key role he played in getting my name on the court.

JOHN STONEBURNER, for his friendship over the years, and for guiding me to Lois Ann Hobbs and recalling that

Davidson College had hired, and then not hired, a Jewish faculty member in the late 1970s (see footnote 12, page 28, of this volume).

JAMES R. STEWART JR., Archives and Special Collections Librarian, F. D. Bluford Library, North Carolina A&T, for providing information about Robert H. Frazier's tenure on the A&T Board of Trustees.

MARK STEIN, for his ongoing support and a lifetime of friendship, but also for coming up with better titles than the ones I planned to use.

JESSIE STARLING, for the incredible leadership that she provided to Save Guilford College, and for the valuable feedback she gave me on an early draft of the epilogue to *Jews, Palestinians, and Friends*. She has earned her place in Alumni Heaven.

NANCY SCHUMAN, for helping me to fill in some gaps in my knowledge about Sam's Jewish background, and for being such a good friend over the years.

ANDREW SAULTERS, for his editorial skills and design magic.

JONATHAN MALINO, for his years of fighting the good fight at Guilford and in the community, and for his help on this project.

BRIAN LAMPKIN, for his encouragement, his invaluable editorial guidance, and his friendship.

MEL KEISER, for his careful reading of the first edition of *Jews, Palestinians, and Friends*, and, especially, for spotting some errors of my account for the era before I came to Guilford.

LOIS ANN HOBBS, for her help in my quest for a photo of Grimsley and Arthur, and for her valuable emailed recollections about Grimsley's early years as President.

JOE GROVES, for taking the time to provide detailed recollections of key events in the 1980s (and for all those good screens he set for me during his years in the geezer game).

MIKE GASPENY, for his steadfast friendship over the years, and for his thoughtful and incisive comments on an early draft of *GEEZERBALL*.

GWEN ERICKSON, for her help over the years on various of my writing projects, including some of the details about Guilford College included in the text of *Jews, Palestinians, and Friends*.

LIZ COOK, for her helpful archival work on the dates of membership for two basketball-playing members of the Guilford Board of Trustees, Bruce Stewart and M. L. Carr.

CRAIG CHAPPELOW, for his ongoing astute analyses of the geezer game, and also for the helpful ideas and editorial suggestions that he gave me, and for his enthusiasm, when I told him about the plans for a book on the game.

KENT CHABOTAR, for that good Presidential decision in 2003.

MAX CARTER, for his quick and thorough responses to my many emailed queries, for his helpful trove of memories, for his good spirit, for his commitment to justice, and for his love of basketball.

TONY BLUETHENTHAL, for his helpful (and tenacious) search for photos of his father and Grimsley Hobbs.

HENRY BERLINER, for his eagle-eye reading of the first edition of *GEEZERBALL* (and his copy-editing corrections) and his good vibes over the years.

KATHY ADAMS, a valued colleague and is a treasured friend, for planting the suggestion, in just the right way and at just the right time, that I write something about the geezer game.

DIYA ABDO, for sharing articles and photos, and for being such a good person.

Lots of others talked to me about their experiences and helped me find information I was seeking, and I want to thank them, too. These include Robert Williams, Katherine Stern Weaver, Karen Spira, Rachel Riskind, Roy Nydorf, Bob Malekoff, Mindy Kutchei, Amal Khoury, Aidan Jones, Jeffrey Janowitz, Heather Hayton, Judith (Judy) Harvey, David Hammond, Vernie Davis, Julie Burke, and Lydia Adelfio.

Index

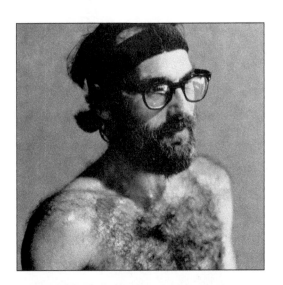

Richie's Court

RICHIE "THE COMMISH" ZWEIGENHAFT

RICHIE ZWEIGENHAFT, Charles A. Dana Professor Emeritus of Psychology at Guilford College, received his BA from Wesleyan University, his MA from Columbia University, and his Ph.D. from the University of California, Santa Cruz. He is the co-author (with G. William Domhoff) of a number of books on diversity in the American power structure and the co-editor (with Eugene Borgida) of a book on collaboration in psychological science.

Made in the USA
Middletown, DE
28 October 2015

CPSIA information can be obtained
at www.ICGtesting.com
Printed in the USA
BVHW051201230223
659070BV00012B/906